PRAISE FOR *LEADING FROM THE FRONT*

"Learning to lead is important for all women. Leadership skills help you make a difference at work, at home and in your community. *Leading from the Front* provides women with ten, relevant principles that will compliment any leadership style."

—Senator Elizabeth Dole

"This engaging book packed with stories from women of courage can help build women with confidence."

—Rosabeth Moss Kanter,
Harvard Business School Professor and
bestselling author of *Confidence:
How Winning Streaks and Losing
Streaks Begin and End*

"The Marine Corps needs a few good women, and in Angie Morgan and Courtney Lynch they obviously got two of the best. *Leading from the Front* is a brilliant, original, practical, profound, human, energetic book written by two remarkable women. It's one of the best books on leadership published in the last several years."

—Tom Peters

"Angie and Courtney are sought after as leadership consultants by many of the top businesses in the country. Now every leader can have access to their inspiring leadership message. *Leading from the Front* provides the reader an insider's view of each woman's experiences in America's ultimate boy's club— the United States Marines."

—Gail Evans,
author of the bestselling business book,
*Play Like a Man, Win Like a
Woman*, and former Executive Vice
President, CNN

"Women and men can benefit tremendously from the leadership skills Angie and Courtney learned as Marines. As a former Marine and a senior executive, I can personally attest that the leadership principles they discuss have been the foundation of my success in the private sector. They have captured the essence of leadership versus management."

—Dave Gagnon,
Senior Vice President,
North America Company Operations
and Training,
Burger King Corporation

"I never thought about women becoming business leaders through joining the Marine Corps, but how terrific that Angie and Courtney not only found and honed their own leadership skills that way, but also codified their learnings for the rest of us. As they tell their very personal experiences and evoke how leadership grows, lesson by lesson, the happy result is that all women benefit from their know-how—without ever having to master the rope climb."

—Betty Spence, Ph.D., President, National Association for Female Executives

LEADING
FROM THE
FRONT

LEADING
FROM THE
FRONT

NO EXCUSE LEADERSHIP
TACTICS FOR WOMEN

ANGIE MORGAN AND COURTNEY LYNCH

McGraw-Hill

New York   Chicago   San Francisco   Lisbon   London   Madrid   Mexico City
Milan   New Delhi   San Juan   Seoul   Singapore   Sydney   Toronto

We dedicate this book to our husbands,
Matthew Morgan and Patrick Lynch,
who inspire us every day.

CONTENTS

CONTENTS

FOREWORD

PAULA ZAHN, CNN

I've always admired the Marine Corps' camaraderie, ethos, and spirit, which is why in 1994 I was curious about what it took to serve in an organization known as "The few. The proud." I wanted to understand the benefits of serving in what is arguably the most demanding branch of the armed forces. I had the unique opportunity to spend a week as a participant in Marine Corps Boot Camp at Parris Island, South Carolina. I was the first female journalist to actively enroll in the rigorous training that all Marine recruits endure. The experience left me with a lasting impression of the dedication, sacrifice, and commitment it takes to earn the title "Marine."

The Marine Corps was very gracious in allowing me to assume the role of Recruit Zahn. I was given no special treatment and completed events right alongside the other women in my training platoon. My drill instructors didn't cut me any slack (even though I happened to be 20 years older than most of the recruits).

Prior to participating in Marine Corps training, I had done my best to prepare for the challenges I would face. New York's Central

Park became my training ground, and I ran about 30 miles per week through its wooded trails, stopping at various playgrounds to test my arm strength on rope swings and monkey bars. I had been an athlete all my life. Training for Boot Camp brought back memories of the demanding drills I went through as a competitive golfer and swimmer in high school and college. Those grueling workouts taught me to approach each new challenge with discipline and thorough preparation. Even after all of this build-up, I was still shocked by the intensity of the physical and mental demands placed on Marine recruits.

During my time at Parris Island, I hiked many miles with a pack, ran in formation runs calling cadence, became familiar with an M-16, and experienced the fear and trepidation of a chemical attack in a gas chamber designed to teach recruits how to use a gas mask properly. I also learned everything from survival swimming to how to employ a grenade. My experience was physically challenging and emotionally daunting. I left the assignment with many bruises, cuts, and scrapes. Even though my body ached for days following my last combat training event, my brief brush with the Corps forever lifted my spirit and confidence.

While the Marine Corps is known for its intense physical training, I quickly learned that there was another aspect of this branch of the armed services that makes it stand out: the people. What was quite amazing to me was the fact that the young women I experienced Boot Camp with had such diverse backgrounds and interests. Some came from small country towns, others from bustling city neighborhoods; some were physically fit, others were not; but all had a strong desire to become Marines. The leadership skills of the drill instructors transformed these many individuals into a strong, cohesive team. By working together to overcome every obstacle Boot Camp placed in front of them, these women became a powerful unit capable of anything.

At Parris Island I also began to recognize the fact that in life we are all conditioned to put limits—both mental and physical—on what we can do. Becoming a leader the Marine Corps way shatters any preconceived limits we have placed on ourselves. As you become a leader here or in the Marines, your confidence soars and your capabilities expand far beyond your belief.

When Angie and Courtney asked me to consider writing the foreword for this book, I was honored to do so because of the deep respect I hold for Marines. While I completed just one week of Boot Camp, Angie and Courtney served a combined 18 years as Marines. I know firsthand how hard they worked to become Marines and how seriously they took their responsibilities as officers. They will tell you that while they learned many lessons through their service, the most effective and relevant lessons were those on leadership.

My most memorable takeaway was an understanding of how the Marine Corps builds and develops its leaders. The Marine Corps believes that all Marines must learn to lead. In order to survive the chaos and uncertainty of war, a Marine is taught how to be decisive, how to take care of others, and how to accept responsibility for his or her actions. The Marine Corps needs leaders who can inspire others and influence outcomes in even the most dire circumstances.

When you think of Boot Camp, you probably picture an angry drill instructor bellowing instructions at recruits. That's a fairly accurate picture, but what you might not understand about that stereotypical scene is the reasons behind the fury. The Corps places recruits under duress not to haze or punish them, but to create an environment of absolute chaos in order to strengthen their resolve and ability to function successfully in stressful situations.

You might wonder how or even if the lessons of Marine Corps training apply to you. I can tell you that they do. As women, we wear many hats and fill many roles. We work hard to balance the demands of our families, our careers, and our involvement in our communities. In order to keep on top of our obligations, we have to be able to manage stress, make good choices, keep our emotions in check, and look out for the needs of others. Surprisingly, these objectives are very similar to the duties of Marine Corps officers. Each day in uniform, Angie and Courtney had to do exactly these things as they led their troops on missions throughout the world. They served successfully as officers because they are outstanding leaders. When they returned to the private sector, they realized they had had a unique education that many of their peers hadn't received. They had been formally trained in leadership, meaning that they had been taught practical ways to lead others, effect change, and bring calm to chaos—things that are important for every woman on her journey to success.

The good news is that you don't need to lace up a pair of combat boots in order to learn to lead the Marine Corps way. In this book, Angie and Courtney have accurately captured the essence of Marine Corps leadership philosophies in 10 easy-to-understand principles. *Leading from the Front* details exactly how you can become a strong leader.

As a journalist, I use leadership skills on a daily basis. Learning to lead was a process that took me many years, but it was immediately enhanced during the training I received at Parris Island. When I completed my assignment with the Marines, I was presented with a hand-painted flag bearing the insignia of the battalion I had proudly served with during training. Receiving that flag was an emotional moment for me because of all it symbolized. The flag hangs in my office today as a reminder of the life-changing experience I had at Parris Island. Every time it catches my eye, I am instantly reminded of the honor, courage, and commitment that Marine leaders possess.

The Marine Corps believes that anyone can become a stronger leader. This theory is proven time and time again as recruits learn how to lead as they strive to earn the title Marine. Angie and Courtney attribute their tremendous ability to meet the challenges and demands of life and career to the leadership lessons they learned in the Marine Corps. I hope you enjoy getting to know them through the stories they share in this book. They truly are "a few good women."

BECOMING MARINES, BECOMING LEADERS

Of the 180,000 warriors in the United States Marine Corps, only about 1,000 are female officers. Much more common a career choice for men than for women, joining the Marine Corps was an unusual move for both of us, but it ultimately presented extraordinary opportunities—opportunities that we could never have foreseen. In addition to strengthening our characters, our minds, and our muscles, the Marine Corps gave us the skills to be successful at whatever we wanted to do. The Corps taught us to be leaders; we now rely on that leadership training every day. But we didn't join the Corps expecting to become leaders. When people hear about our unusual career path, their first question is almost always, "Why?" "Why would two young women with so many options choose to join America's elite fighting force?"

ALL-AMERICAN CHILDHOODS

Growing up, we were typical all-American girls. We played dress up, read *Sweet Valley High* books, rode bikes, and had slumber parties with our friends. We were energetic and liked to seek out new challenges.

While we weren't particularly gifted or unusual, there were some signs early on that we had the makings of Marines.

Angie enjoyed outdoor adventures during the summer with her family, spending many weekends crammed into their small boat touring Lake Michigan. An athletic child, her free time during the school year was full of running races, dance classes, music lessons, and homework. She was competitive and enjoyed calling the shots, and she was elected president of her school's student government.

I, Courtney, also enjoyed adventures and sports; falling in love with horses at a young age, I spent most of my free moments caring for other people's animals in exchange for the chance to ride them. While most of my girlfriends liked dressage, the controlled form of horseback riding, I loved cross-country—essentially a race at breakneck speed through the countryside, jumping over natural and man-made obstacles. I was a self-assured kid, which is why I had no qualms about joining boys' sports teams. I was one of the first girls to try out for the Fairfax City Little League "Majors" and earned a spot on the competitive AAA team.

High School Hijinks

By high school, I was like most other teens my age: active in sports, on the cheerleading squad, and dating boys on the weekend. I wasn't a model student, but after freshman year my grades and focus improved. At that point I began looking beyond high school and was aiming for a successful career and a comfortable lifestyle.

Where I started buckling down during high school, Angie began breaking free of her parents' close monitoring. Although always a good student, she also had a rebellious streak. In addition to her unorthodox dress—including dying her hair bright auburn, wearing flannel shirts, and Doc Martin boots with dresses—she also discovered recreational drinking. Although her parents were initially unaware of her behavior, they quickly caught on after Angie returned from a night of partying with friends. That's when they laid down the law about college, and when Angie's Marine Corps future suddenly emerged.

Anchor's Aweigh! Naval ROTC–bound

Angie's dad wasn't excited about the prospect of paying for an expensive college if she was going to party her way through it, so he gave her two options: register at a local community college and live at home, or go to her dream school, the University of Michigan, as a member of the Naval ROTC (Reserve Officers Training Corps) for the first semester. Unwilling to turn down the chance to attend the U of M, Angie opted to join ROTC, although she was sure she would hate it. She was right, at first.

Military training had not been part of her college plans at all, and she intended to have a very short military career. Getting up at 5:00 a.m. several mornings a week, polishing her shoes and brass buckles, and marching around campus were not what she wanted to be doing. During the first few weeks of military training, she called her parents frequently to complain about some aspect of it. But then Major Samuel White,* the Marine Officer Instructor at ROTC, took Angie aside and told her she was a prime candidate for a Marine Corps officer position. He felt that her extensive physical abilities and competitive nature would make her a natural choice for the Corps, which so far had no other women entering the program that year. It wasn't for her, Angie tried to tell him. She had made a one-semester commitment to the military in order to appease her father, but she had no intention of continuing in the program.

"What do you plan to do with your life?" Major White asked her. "Be an English teacher," she told him. "You can always be a teacher," he said. "How many other opportunities will you have to be a Marine?" He told her that the Corps wasn't about buzz cuts, guns, and tattoos— it was about honor, courage, and commitment. It was also about a sense of belonging, something Angie had been missing since arriving on

---

*All names have been fictionalized.

campus. After speaking to Major White, Angie began to notice the future Marines in her unit. They were extremely professional, dedicated to service, and committed to success. They also looked out for one another and had a strong sense of camaraderie. She was missing her family, and had not yet developed her own set of friends, and the close-knit group of students who planned to be Marines was what she had been looking for—what she needed.

At the end of her first semester, much to the amazement of her parents, Angie was ready to sign up voluntarily for the Marine Corps. Three years later she graduated at the top of her class, earning the title Battalion Commander—(the student leader of all the officers in training), and was commissioned a second lieutenant.

Focused Journalism Student

My college years, on the other hand, were a bit different. I enjoyed my life as a sorority sister at North Carolina State University; military service couldn't have been further from my mind. In fact, I felt sorry for the ROTC kids I'd see on campus, who had to wear uniforms even on the hottest days and carry heavy backpacks at their sides. My days were spent balancing time with friends and work at the local ABC affiliate with my many classes. I juggled an average of 18 credit hours each semester with work at the TV station and various other part-time jobs. Always trying to gain an advantage, I graduated a semester ahead of my classmates. My goal at the time was to become a broadcast journalist, although I also planned to earn a law degree to make me a better-rounded reporter.

After graduation, I moved to Aspen, Colorado, where I spent my days skiing and my nights working as an on-air personality at a very small TV station. During my free time, I worked on my law school applications, setting my sights on the University of Virginia, my dream school, or the College of William and Mary. Unfortunately, I wasn't accepted by either of them. My remaining options were Seton Hall and Creighton University.

After landing a job at the CBS affiliate in Omaha, I settled on Creighton, where I could study law and have a broadcast job that would help cover my living expenses. But when I learned that I would need to borrow $96,000 to pay for law school, I began to question whether taking large loans to attend an out-of-state school was my best move. Maybe I should focus on making myself distinctive—impressive even—as a law school candidate so that I might be admitted to UVA or William and Mary on a second try.

I became focused on finding a way to pay for law school while gaining life experience. At the same time, I started to notice news stories about the military. It dawned on me that a military career could provide both the money for law school and the experience I needed to potentially qualify for a top university; also, it would make me a better, more qualified journalist and give me an opportunity to serve my country. The military was the "more" I needed. So I started calling military recruiting offices to inquire about officer training. The Navy told me the waiting period for taking a skills assessment test was six weeks. Unwilling to wait, I called the Marine Corps, which was able to consider me that week. I had narrowed my choices to those two branches because the fathers of two of my friends had served in them, but I really knew very little about what I was in for. I was going with my gut.

Captain Jake Franklin, the Marine recruiter I met with, made it clear that becoming a Marine wouldn't be easy. The side of me that loves a challenge was intrigued by the fact that Captain Franklin offered me no guarantee of making it through the training. That spurred my competitive spirit. But before he put me on the slate for Officer Candidate School (OCS), Captain Franklin wanted me to prepare physically for the training. I had only four months. I immediately hired a personal trainer to help improve my arm hang time from 12 seconds to 70 seconds, the standard for women, and the number of sit-ups I could comfortably do in two minutes from 20 to 80. I also trained to run three miles—the initial distance Marine recruits are required to complete. To pay for all of this training I took a job as a waitress at a local restaurant, working nights as I spent my days in the gym.

A couple of months before my scheduled departure date, the immensity of this decision hit me. What was I doing, I wondered?! I was scared and nervous. This was the biggest challenge I'd ever faced, and, unlike in past situations, I wasn't so sure I'd be successful here. But I couldn't turn back. I was taking a leap of faith—the first of many in the Corps.

THE FEW, THE PROUD

Marine Corps training lives up to its reputation as tough and painful, but it also makes you stronger in so many ways. It takes a lot of work to become a Marine officer. First, all officers must have a college degree. Next is Officer Candidate School (OCS), essentially boot camp for officers. After OCS, all new lieutenants complete six months of infantry training at The Basic School (TBS), which is the last hurdle before you're eligible to command troops. This comprehensive program is a critical step for all officers, during which you receive thousands of hours of instruction, endure countless evaluations to improve your performance, and come away extremely knowledgeable about infantry tactics. But, ultimately, you learn even more about yourself and your capabilities than you learn about the infantry itself.

It was during this time that Angie and I met. We were both sitting in the back of a bus on the way to land navigation training at TBS in Quantico, which involved the complex art of finding boxes hidden deep in the woods with only a compass and map to guide you—standard fare at TBS. Without really thinking, we sat next to each other, and then laughed when we realized we were the only women on the bus. It was a long trip out to the test site, and we found comfort in talking to each other about the grueling training we were enduring, as well as our fears and concerns. That fateful bus ride was the beginning of an amazing friendship.

Once we completed our land navigation exam, the Marine Corps presented even more challenges. Hiking 20 miles with backpacks became routine, and learning how to conduct combat assaults became second nature. At every turn, our bodies and minds were pushed to their limits. But we made a commitment to help each other make it. After training, we were both assigned to the DOD's Defense Information School for 10 weeks to learn how to be public affairs officers (PAOs). Our friendship continued to grow as we spent time together in and out of the classroom. We then parted ways—Angie to Hawaii and I to Japan—but kept in touch via e-mail and phone calls from our Marine Corps bases. Our regular contact continued even after we left active-duty service, but instead of commiserating about military assignments, we'd often talk about our new business careers—Angie's in L.A. and mine in Washington, D.C. Life in the civilian world was certainly different from life in the Marine Corps. At that point our personal lives were also getting more interesting. We both became engaged around the same time, and we were excited about the new direction our lives were taking.

Despite the challenges of our early days in uniform, we went on to achieve considerable success in the Corps. We led units as large as 50, deployed throughout the world, and by the time we left the Corps, we were both accomplished officers: I received two Navy Achievement Medals and the Joint Commendation Medal for my superior service, and Angie was awarded a Certificate of Commendation and the Navy Commendation Medal. We both left active duty as successful officers, anticipating successful private-sector careers. We weren't disappointed.

We were strong performers in the Corps and later in the business world because of the leadership training we had received, not because of some special talent we already had. But the fact that we did earn the title of Marine—as officers, no less—is proof that anyone can learn how to be a leader.

ACKNOWLEDGMENTS

We'd like to thank Marcia Layton-Turner; without her tremendous abilities, patience, support, and dedication, this book would not have been possible. We'd also like to thank our agent, Lorin Rees, for his persistence and commitment to our project. We also extend our appreciation to our fantastic editor, Jeanne Glasser, who added a valuable perspective to our work.

We'd like to express our gratitude for our wonderful families and supportive friends who have given us sound advice and a kind ear throughout every twist and turn of our writing journey. We'd like to thank Lynn Anne Christensen, Whitney Hopler (an author we deeply admire), Liz Lamirand, Marilyn Judge, Laura Salapka, and Susan Stoner for the time they spent reading our early drafts and providing us with great feedback. Their contributions truly made this a better book.

There have been some key men and women in our lives who have exemplified the phrase "leading from the front." Thank you, Jenni Amoe, Chandra Cox, Liz Cranston, Kathy Kobe, Mary Fran Love,

Mark Meinschein, Chris Parker, Kathy Roth-Douquet, Doris Turner, and Karin Williams for your leadership.

Finally, we'd like to thank the following Navy and Marine Corps leaders for the profound impact they have made on our lives: Larry Ammerman, Vinny Coglianese, Chris Cortez, Rhys Evans, Ed Floeter, John French, Fred Geier, Tom Gross, Byron Harper, Jerry Judge, Bob Lee, Al Moore, Jeff Nyhart, Doug Personious, Mastin Robeson, Dan Ryan, Cliff Stanley, Kim Steinport, Bob Turner, Sam Whidhelm, Bill Whitlow, and John Williams. Semper Fi!

INTRODUCTION

Some employees who attend our leadership workshops are there under duress; they arrive skeptical that the time spent in training will be worth their while. Karen was no different.

Karen attended a leadership workshop that we conducted for a large restaurant chain in Phoenix, Arizona. Her boss had gathered his team together for a national conference, and Karen had no choice but to participate in this session. However, spending three hours in leadership training was really not something she wanted to do that afternoon.

When Karen arrived at the hotel conference room, her mind was elsewhere—running through a long list of things she needed to get done at work. She hated these meetings because they never seemed to accomplish anything or teach her anything new. Plus, work was really crazy, and she was having a tough time juggling her job and her family. She had also recently been passed over for a key promotion, and she was still struggling to understand why. Her manager had told her that she just didn't seem ready for the added responsibility. Perhaps more experience would prepare her, she was told. Karen was doubtful; she'd been in her current position for close to six years, what more experience did she need? She understood the job well and had mastered the technical aspects of the job; what else did she need to learn in order to become a manager?! Then her mind wandered to her teenage son, who had been spending time with a group of kids who were into skipping school, smoking, and drinking. Karen was worried about him but wasn't sure what she should (or could) do.

She sat down in the back of the room and casually leafed through the workshop materials, noticing that the presenters for the workshop were two former Marines. "Great," she thought. "What can I possibly learn from two guys who were in the military?" She had no interest in the military, or in hearing theories about how work is like war and how having a "take no prisoners" attitude can help.

The lights dimmed and the workshop began. We appeared on stage. Our youthful looks gave Karen the impression that we were the warm-up act, getting the audience ready for the two Marines. Then we began talking about our time in the trenches and showed photos of ourselves in camouflage on the conference room screens. Surprised, Karen began to listen more intently.

As we talked about the need to be decisive, Karen began to recall circumstances at work where she had had a hard time making decisions. She hadn't realized that being decisive had anything to do with demonstrating an ability to lead. We also emphasized the importance of accepting responsibility before blaming others, and Karen winced as she recognized her tendency to point the finger at others before questioning whether she had any responsibility for the problem; she thought about how she had blamed her boss when she was passed over for promotion, when, really, it could have had something to do with her.

As the workshop continued, we explained how we had learned to think before acting, especially before overreacting. We went on to explain that a leader who loses her cool each time she gets bad news never gets the full story. Karen thought of her son and how she had often reacted by flying off the handle when she caught him breaking his curfew. Now her son and she were barely speaking. "Wow! That makes sense." No wonder her son clammed up every time she tried to talk to him; he expected her to launch into another tirade.

Karen hadn't realized how damaging some aspects of her behavior were to her career and her home life—she thought they were just part of her personality. Now she could see how her behavior was getting in the way of her progress. She needed to be more of a leader.

The workshop hours flew by. Not normally one to speak up in a conference, Karen volunteered to answer several of the questions we posed to the audience. At the end of the workshop, she approached us and thanked us for our insights. One of us gave Karen a business card, and we told her we looked forward to her keeping in touch.

LEADERSHIP LESSONS

Karen did keep in touch. She kept us posted as she worked to improve her performance in the office, especially as she developed the courage to take more initiative. She began to anticipate the needs of others in her office and to look for opportunities to assist coworkers with difficult tasks. About six months after attending our presentation, she was offered a promotion to a job more senior than the one she had originally been denied.

Karen also told us that her relationship with her son had dramatically improved. She tried hard not to lose her temper with him; instead, she tried to encourage an ongoing dialogue. She created a climate in which honest, calm communication could take place. Karen also told us that she had never thought of herself as a leader, but when she realized that leadership was a role that had nothing to do with a job title, she saw that she could be a leader in many areas of her life. By setting a positive example and being able to meet the standards she expected from others, she was not only leading her own life, but also leading her colleagues and peers.

From Arizona to Arkansas to Michigan to New York, experiences like Karen's take place at every training session we lead. We founded Lead Star, our leadership consulting company, in order to spark a national dialogue on the topic of women and leadership. Being a leader has nothing to do with your job title, salary, pay grade, the number of people who report to you, or your department's budget. Yet in the leadership consulting we do, that's often how participants initially define leaders—by their perks and their power. True, many leaders do earn promotions, pay increases, and recognition for a job well done, but that's merely a by-product of strong leadership skills.

The world's top companies have leaders at every level of the organization. Corporations are now recognizing the value of leadership training for all their employees as a way of achieving larger-scale success. As a result, we have been approached to teach employees the specifics of becoming leaders. In the past year alone, Lead Star has consulted with organizations like Wal-Mart, Burger King, Raytheon, Baxter International, the Girls Scouts of America, and Baylor College of Medicine, among others. And our message has touched a nerve. We know this because in addition to our consulting engagements, we also have been featured in some of the nation's best-known newspapers and magazines, including the *New York Times, Fast Company,* and *Inc.* We've made live appearances on top TV networks, such as CNN, CNBC, and Fox News, and have been given many other media opportunities.

Our experiences behind the military firing lines helped us differentiate between true leaders and wanna-be's. As Marines, we saw what worked and what didn't in life-and-death situations. Then we took what we had learned and applied it to our own lives in corporate America, where we achieved success rather quickly. But this book is not about how to become a Marine. This book is about how to become a leader.

You may never have thought that being a leader is important, but we're here to tell you why it is and how to become one. Leadership skills are the solutions that women need to succeed, though most don't know it. Women need to understand how their behavior affects their promotion potential, and to see how small changes in their attitude can have big payoffs. That's what our book does—it teaches women how to make behavioral changes that can vastly improve their careers and their lives.

Leading from the Front will give you tools and skills that will let you be more productive, less stressed, more successful, and more in control of your professional and personal lives. We are a testament to the power of these leadership lessons. Throughout this book you'll hear from both of us as we take turns telling our stories, sharing what we've learned that has worked for us, and showing how it can work for you, both on the job and in your personal life. Although we share a common bond of leadership training in the Marine Corps, we each have our own unique experiences. For that reason, you'll hear from us individually about our successes, our failures, and the important principles we learned that we teach to women all over the country.

LEAD STAR'S 10 LEADERSHIP PRINCIPLES

Leadership comes down to behavior, but few women understand how their behavior can help or hurt their career. Lead Star's Leadership Principles were developed from our experience applying the leadership lessons acquired in the Corps to everyday life in the business world and beyond. Using these principles, these tactics, every day can transform your life. They aren't difficult to understand, but they do take effort to practice.

5

1. Meet and exceed the standards you ask of others—lead from the front

2. Make timely decisions—find the 80 percent solution

3. Seek to take responsibility before you begin to place blame

4. True leaders dedicate themselves to service—take care of those you lead

5. Think before you act—especially before you overreact

6. When faced with a crisis—aviate, navigate, communicate

7. Courage + initiative + perseverance + integrity = success

8. Don't cry over something that won't cry over you

9. Say you're sorry only when you're at fault

10. Always lead as you are.

When you use them regularly, you'll be amazed at the difference these principles can make in your professional and personal relationships—they'll affect your productivity, your attitude, and your reputation. The impact that leadership behavior can make was never clearer for Courtney than during an overseas assignment in Indonesia, when she ran into trouble; her leadership know-how made the difference between a potentially deadly encounter and a peaceful roadside interaction.

THE LEADERSHIP ADVANTAGE

Courtney

"Is not a problem," Budi, our slender, dark-haired driver assured us in broken English. He smiled a mouthful of bad teeth and told us that he knew the way to Surabaya, a city on the eastern coast of

Indonesia. The three of us—Budi; Sergeant Miller, a combat correspondent; and I—had left the American base camp just a couple of hours before to make our flight back to Okinawa, Japan, our home base. But an hour into the hot and sticky drive, our SUV lost sight of the other cars in the convoy, and we were meandering the dusty, barren roads alone, trusting that Budi knew the way. Then we heard a loud bang, and the car suddenly lurched sideways. One of our tires was flat. Our empty trunk revealed that we had no spare, so Budi went to get one, 10 miles away.

It was late in the afternoon, the road had been baking all day in the searing heat, and Sergeant Miller and I were standing by our shiny, new Range Rover somewhere along the coast. We didn't know the area or the language and were unarmed, thanks to having flown in on a commercial airline that prohibits personal weapons. Of course, now I regretted not having made other travel arrangements.

I had spent the last two weeks in the Kerang Tekak section of East Java, Indonesia, documenting the construction of several town halls, community centers, schools, roadways, and sewer system enhancements that Marines were completing for the constantly typhoon-threatened country. As a Marine Corps public affairs officer, I photographed, filmed, and wrote about the Corps' work in the region for network television coverage back home. Our work promoting human rights and public safety is key to developing goodwill here, in a country that spans two strategic maritime straits in the Indian Ocean and Persian Gulf.

Indonesia is also a very poor country. The rural areas have dirt roads, the houses are lean-tos, and food is scarce. Most people travel by oxcart, and the few cars on the roads are old and worn. And here we were standing by a shiny new $50,000 SUV, loaded with $125,000 of camera equipment—worth more than what some local residents would earn in a lifetime. We were easy targets for desperate citizens, and we knew it.

After we moved the Range Rover to the side of the road, the sergeant and I decided to take a look around. We didn't get very far because a crowd gathered almost immediately. First there were 10, then 20, then 30 or more men and women who came from the local village up the road and from houses (huts really) tucked away behind the dry shrubbery. The men were dressed in lightweight, Western-style clothing: navy or brown workpants with worn and faded short-sleeved, button-down shirts. The women wore traditional sarongs and tops, all in muted earth tones. They were calm, but intent, and they had careful eyes on me. I made out a few words in Bahasa Indonesia, the local language, and sensed their fascination with me—a white, blonde, green-eyed woman in a military uniform.

I was probably the first female Marine Corps officer the Indonesians had ever seen. Standing 5'8" in black lace-up combat boots, green camouflage pants, matching shirt, and cap, I was several inches taller than most Indonesian men. My hair, eyes, and fair skin also stood out among their dark features. Although the villagers had probably seen Marines, since a detachment of about 50 U.S. military personnel was in the region as part of the humanitarian project I had been filming, a white woman—let alone a white woman in uniform—was rare.

The quickly gathering crowd made us nervous, as the area was known for antigovernment sentiment and rebellious activity. Just a few months before, 1,200 civilians had died during riots in Jakarta, and rioters had only recently set a building and two cars on fire nearby, in central Java. As I stood there and smiled at the crowd, saying hello, I was mentally reviewing my Marine Corps training for possible strategies to get us out of there unharmed. As the senior officer, I was responsible for the safety of Sergeant Miller and our equipment. I had to protect them.

At The Basic School (TBS) in Quantico, Virginia, where I was introduced to Marine Corps infantry tactics and trained in hand-to-hand combat, I had learned how to fight with my bare hands, a knife, or an M-16 rifle. I had been trained to defend myself and my troops, but I had also been taught to analyze complex situations before taking action. Months of intense leadership training had demonstrated to me the importance of being decisive in order to gain the upper hand in chaotic situations. I watched the crowd for any indications of its intentions.

I would have felt safer with our driver's pistol at my side, but it was locked away on the floor of the car, where he had placed it for safekeeping before beginning his trek for the replacement tire. We had no weapons, and locking ourselves in the Range Rover seemed foolish at this point.

Sweat dripped from my head and face as I struggled to stay cool in uniform. Steam rose from the road and met the sun's scorching rays, strangling us with heat and humidity. It was 90 degrees, and we couldn't leave the car to find shade. Dehydrated, Sergeant Miller reached for a drink of water from a clear plastic bottle in the back of the SUV. Having been baking in the sun for a couple of hours, the bottle was hot to the touch. Desperate, the sergeant took a big swig from it, but as soon as he tasted the scalding water, he spat it out. It was putrid.

He reached back into the SUV, into the remains of a military-issued meal, and grabbed a package of powdered grape drink mix that the military distributes to cover up the taste and smell of foul water. He tore it open, poured it into the water bottle, and shook it. The crowd grew silent, watching the bottle turn from clear to purple. They were mesmerized. Sergeant Miller had turned water into wine.

I spotted my opening. The locals were focused on the drink, and we needed to keep their attention there. Eager to change their mood and their intentions, I immediately directed the sergeant to mix up the rest of the grape drink mix we had in the trunk. As soon as the crowd recognized that we were going to share the drink, the tension broke, and they giggled and chatted. Instead of sparking a violent outbreak, we opened up a roadside Kool-Aid stand. The quick thinking I'd learned in the Corps, through the hundreds of decision-making tests, made all the difference. Now, instead of focusing on me and our fully loaded Range Rover, the crowd was transfixed by Sergeant Miller's "magic."

The villagers shuffled into a single line, hoping to sample the "wine." One by one, they stepped up, took a small mouthful, and smiled. For the next 20 or 30 minutes, we let the crowd take sips of the grape drink until our driver returned with a new tire. It took less than five minutes to swap the tires and make our getaway.

Thanks to my leadership training, we were safe. Had I not developed the ability to deal with crises, think on my feet, and look for opportunities to meet the needs of those involved, who knows what might have happened? Had I not taken action to try to influence what happened next, even when I didn't know what the villagers were thinking, we would have been at their mercy. My being a leader may have saved our lives. Later, that same training would help shape my private-sector career.

Looking back, I can see why the crowd gathered and stared at me. In Indonesia, where women are near-second-class citizens who are rarely in the public eye, the sight of a woman in uniform must have been shocking. Few Indonesian women are in leadership positions, and none are in the military. I was surely a spectacle, a curiosity to them.

Just as I was an oddity to the local Indonesians, I was also a curiosity to my fellow troops in the U.S. military. Of the 1,425,887 active-duty service people in the armed forces—Army, Navy, Air Force, and Marines—213,224 (or 15 percent) are women. But only 34,796 women—or 2.5 percent—are commissioned officers who have reached the ranks of management within the armed forces.

And the Marine Corps, where I served, has the fewest women of all the armed forces: In September 2003, there were 75,000 women in the Army, 70,000 in the Air Force, and close to 55,000 in the Navy.˙ Only 10,664 women were serving in the Marine Corps. And of the 10,664 women Marines, only 1,000—less than 1 percent of the entire Marine Corps—were officers. Angie Morgan and I were two of the rarest members of the U.S. military—captains in the Marine Corps. During our service as Marines, there were exactly 300 female captains, and only 155 women ranked above us. We were among the very few women in the world to have received leadership training from the U.S. Marine Corps, where men are clearly the majority. Armed with this information, we've achieved success in the corporate world in a relatively short period of time. In this book we'll share the same exact leadership lessons with you so that you can apply these teachings to your own career and personal life.

APPLYING MARINE LESSONS
TO LIFE AFTER THE CORPS

Angie

To win every fight and prepare for any event, the Marine Corps instills recruits with leadership skills from the very beginning. The harsh reality of the battlefield is that any commanding officer can die suddenly. And if each Marine isn't trained and prepared to step up when the troop leader is killed in action, other Marines will die, and the battle will be lost. The most valuable lessons we learned as Marines weren't how to fire a rifle or how to destroy the enemy. The most valued and lasting lessons were how to lead others to victory. In the Corps, we learned how to make split-second decisions based on minimal information, the importance of meeting the standards we held our troops to, and how to improve our team's performance by addressing the individual needs of each of its members. We also learned how to listen, how to command, and how to protect.

When we left active-duty service years later, we settled into our new lives as ordinary citizens, accepting challenging positions with respected companies. Except we weren't ordinary citizens, we soon discovered. We knew that our Marine Corps service made us different, but we didn't know how different until we reentered civilian life. Then we saw firsthand the advantage we had as trained leaders. Our leadership skills served us well in the business world from day one. In Courtney's first year as a sales manager, she generated more than $30 million in sales revenue for the software developer she worked for, or 126 percent of her sales quota. I was responsible for $23 million in pharmaceutical sales for my employer, which contributed to my team's national sales awards. In a matter of months, we rose to the top of our departments, where others had been working for years without similar success.

We also started to investigate what made us so different. Why weren't more women having the same success? We learned that it all came down to leadership. Many women aren't leading their own lives. We frequently notice women at work who say yes to additional commitments when they should have said no because they already have too much to do. And by accepting additional work when they don't really have the time, they end up either doing a lower-quality job or sacrificing other aspects of their job or their life to get the work done. In many cases, they're at the mercy of their commitments. Between trying to be better employees, better managers, better moms, better wives, better citizens, better children, and better housekeepers, many women feel that their lives aren't their own. Their workday stretches from morning until night, they have little time for family and friends, their work is seemingly never done, they can't find time to exercise, and they barely have time for themselves. They're doing so much that they're struggling to balance their work and personal roles, and they often feel that they're failing.

To survive, many women have developed coping mechanisms to get them through the day. Because they're so overburdened, they nearly break down in tears at work when things go awry; they blame others for problems, deflecting responsibility for failure; they're out of shape, yet make excuses for not eating right and not exercising; and they avoid confrontation, hoping that conflicts will "work themselves out." Understandably, they avoid taking responsibility, avoid additional work, and avoid tackling situations head on. They're too stressed and overworked. Yet these coping mechanisms don't help in the long term; they just cause more difficulties. The solution is to get out from under these excuses and learn to lead your life and the lives of those around you. To take charge of the situations you find yourself in, you need to be a leader.

The lessons we learned, the tools we gained, and the life strategies we adopted in the Corps can be applied to further your career and manage your life. We have taken the Corps' leadership philosophies and translated them into 10 principles that will guide you on your journey to becoming a leader.

For instance, after hearing the principle "courage + initiative + perseverance = success," one shy Burger King employee resolved to speak up once a week at staff meetings to share her perspective. The response to her increased participation was so positive that she now frequently speaks up and has been rewarded with additional assignments and recognition. Another employee, this one from Wal-Mart, told us she used to apologize for everything. "If it was raining in the morning, I'd apologize to my employees for their having to get wet walking in," she says. But now, after learning the importance of apologizing only when you're at fault, she's much more solutions-oriented rather than problem-oriented, and her productivity has soared. And a financial services employee who used to blame others for her slow professional progress finally took responsibility for her career and is now hotly recruited by two major firms. Even if you apply only one or two of the principles we discuss in this book and through our consulting, you'll be amazed by the positive results you'll begin to see.

We'd go one step further and say that being a leader will change your life. You'll spot opportunities everywhere to influence outcomes and inspire others. You'll also see yourself differently—as the capable, strong woman you are. Becoming a leader will give you the courage and confidence to pursue opportunities for change, to do what you need to do to get the life you deserve. That may mean pursuing a significant promotion or a job with new responsibilities, or perhaps owning your own business. Leadership skills will show you how to move your life in the direction you want it to go. *Leading from the Front* gives you all the tools you need to make this happen.

CHAPTER 1

MEET AND EXCEED THE STANDARDS YOU ASK OF OTHERS—LEAD FROM THE FRONT

True leaders are less concerned about the rewards of being a leader and more aware of the responsibility that the role brings—the responsibility for serving as a role model to those around them. In other words, direct reports do not a leader make. We have seen managers with huge staffs fail miserably at leading their teams and have to endure high turnover and poor performance from their employees. On the other hand, we've witnessed people without management responsibility whom others in the department looked to for guidance and direction—an administrative assistant, an executive receptionist, and a newly promoted sales rep. They were achieving results for their employer despite the fact that they hadn't officially been designated leaders. Titles really don't define leaders; behavior and attitude make the difference.

You may not have official reports—people who answer to you—at work, at school, or at home. Nonetheless, you can still be a leader.

Some of the audiences we've spoken to have been somewhat skeptical about this, wondering aloud why they needed to try to be leaders when they had no obvious followers. What was the point? Our response was that leadership isn't based on formalized or official reporting structures; anyone and everyone around you may be looking to you to show them how to be successful. Leaders are role models; some are official and some are unofficial, but they can all have a major influence on their organization's success. And if you contribute to your company's success, you're much more likely to be recognized and rewarded for your role, perhaps with a promotion, additional responsibilities, more money, more perks, more scheduling flexibility—you name it. By helping to lead your company, you can also take greater control of your own career and success.

Striving to be your best, upholding your organization's performance standards, and treating others with respect are likely to earn you followers. But you may not recognize those who are looking to you to set an example. A college intern in your department, your colleague down the hall, a neighbor's child, the waitress at your favorite restaurant—they all may be silently looking to you for inspiration and guidance in living their lives, making it that much more important that you always strive to do your best.

Leaders set the tone for their followers, demonstrating in thought, word, and deed how others are expected to behave. They enforce company policy rather than interpreting it as they see fit. Those who ignore the rules unwittingly set a bad example for other employees, such as a coworker who blatantly ignores company guidelines on reimbursable expenses. Not only are they acting unethically, but also they are sending a message to their employees that they can interpret company guidelines however they want. This is not leadership behavior.

It's easy to spot people who aren't leaders. They expect others to treat them with respect, but don't behave in a manner that warrants it. They say they want to build strong, trustworthy teams, but gossip about teammates behind their backs. They want positive affirmation and encouragement, but provide only insults and criticism to their staff. They just can't understand why others aren't treating them the way they expect to be treated. The problem is that they aren't leading from the front. If you're not leading from the front, you aren't setting a higher standard and establishing how you expect those around you to behave. Leading from the back of the pack means that you've relinquished control over your team and are much less likely to be successful.

The meaning of the phrase "leading from the front" seemed pretty obvious when we first heard it during Marine Corps training. Of course leaders are out in front—where else would they be?! By definition, to be a leader, you need to have people following you. But as we became part of the Corps, we recognized that the phrase was much more than an observation about where leaders should position themselves. It's about setting standards and meeting those that are set for you—leaders are the keepers of the standards. It's about striving to be your best at any task you undertake. Leading from the front epitomizes the culture of the Marine Corps.

The Corps lives and dies by a set of standards. And it is those exacting standards that make the Marine Corps the elite fighting force it is today. The Corps' high standards apply to everything job-related—from continuing education, to the use of technology, to knowledge of the latest combat capabilities. Even something as basic as how to wear a Marine Corps uniform has clear guidelines—every medal, every insignia, and every button on a uniform must be worn in a precise location, specified to the millimeter.

Despite its Marine Corps roots, leading from the front is a concept that applies equally well in the private sector. True leaders constantly strive to do their best, and lead by doing—by modeling the behavior they want to engender in others.

STRIVE FOR RESPECT BASED ON PERFORMANCE, NOT TITLE OR RANK

Courtney

Early in my military career, I didn't know I needed to be led. In the Marine Corps chain of command, a second lieutenant, which I was, has seniority over a gunnery sergeant. But that seniority is simply a rank—it does not make a leader. Despite my officer status, I was not ready to lead. I had completed officer training, but I still had a lot to learn. Fortunately, the Marine Corps routinely assigns new lieutenants a mentor to help shape them into stronger leaders. It is the role of a gunnery sergeant to serve as advisor and confidante to new officers, balancing the lieutenants' enthusiasm and officer training with their own years of experience. After stress fracturing my hip during officer training, I was sidelined for several months to undergo physical therapy before completing additional infantry training at The Basic School. Translation: I was given a desk job at recruiting command.

Because of my broadcast journalism experience, I was assigned the task of creating and producing a recruiting video for female Marine Corps officers. This I could do, I thought! My challenge was marshaling the resources needed to research, film, write, and edit the video in just a couple of months. Since most of the work required a skilled videographer, I decided to recruit the best one in the Marine Corps to help me, especially since there was no way I could get all of the work done on my own. I soon learned that the Marine Corps' top videographer, Gunnery Sergeant Tom Gerhart, was stationed nearby in Washington, D.C. Now all I had to do was convince him to help me produce the video.

His first reaction to my telephone plea for help was to politely decline. He was a 16-year veteran of the Corps and an award-winning videographer, and I was a newly minted 20-something officer. He didn't want to work with a rookie. I understood, but I really needed his help. I managed to persuade him by demonstrating that I knew a thing or two about video production. He wouldn't have to hold my hand. I told him that this would be a very visible assignment that could be good for his career—the project was a high-priority task that had the backing of a two-star general. So, after a bit of arm-twisting on my part, we finally headed out together for boot camp at Parris Island, South Carolina, the Marine Corps' East Coast training center, to begin work.

I had been an officer for all of six weeks. I had heard all about the importance of leading from the front—of being a role model—during training. I grasped the concept, but it was obvious to Gunny Gerhart that while I might have understood what the words meant, I didn't understand why leading from the front was important. I had learned many new things, but I wasn't always sure how to pull them all together. Gunny showed me how. He began his mentoring with my uniform.

I had memorized the regulations for wearing the Marine Corps uniform, which were extensive and specific, and I followed them, sort of. My uniform was generally pressed, my sleeves were rolled as required, and my insignia were approximately where they should be, but my brass was often dull and my boots, though not scuffed, didn't reflect light the way they should. I didn't pay as much attention to my appearance as I could have. I met the standard, barely. Gunny saw that, and that's where he started his mentoring.

"I think you're going to be a good officer," he told me early in the trip, which was the gunny's way of subtly letting me know that I wasn't there yet. During our first week on the road, at the end of the day, he asked for my uniform. "Why don't I show you how a leader wears her uniform?" he asked. It wasn't really a request; it was more of a command. I gladly handed it over, eager to learn from a master.

"Do you know how many hours the recruits at Parris Island spend prepping their uniform, Lieutenant?" he asked. I had no idea. "A dress uniform takes at least three hours to prepare correctly," he told me. "How do you think it would look if you showed up on base wearing a uniform that looked like crap?" Ouch, that stung, but I knew right away that he was right. I wasn't working hard enough to be an example. "You're their superior. You're a leader. You're supposed to be leading from the front. They've been taught to look to you for guidance. How do you think they would feel about the Marine Corps if they saw a lieutenant in such a poorly prepped uniform? The way you wear your uniform shows your pride in all that the Marine Corps stands for. And if you don't have that pride, how can you expect your Marines to?!"

He then pressed it perfectly, folded my sleeves expertly, put my rank insignia in their proper positions, and shined my boots to a high-gloss finish. While he worked, he explained the meaning of each insignia, telling me stories that further boosted my pride in being a Marine. He also explained how being a leader starts with your appearance, your attitude. Rather than lecturing me, he made me *want* to wear my uniform absolutely perfectly. Then he gave it back. I appreciated the responsibility of my officer status the next time I put it on.

Rank is everything at Parris Island. Officers are treated like gods by the men and women in training, who are taught to follow their lead. I was somewhat oblivious to this as I walked down the sidewalk to a meeting later that week. But that day was a turning point for me as an officer.

There were about 65 men headed down the street toward me. I could hear the stomp of their boots hitting the pavement in unison. I noticed the platoon, admired its uniformity and precision, and kept walking. Suddenly, the men came to a screeching halt. All 130 boots were silenced in an instant. They snapped to attention, rifles at their side, faces forward. I looked around to find out whom they were saluting.

It took a few seconds, but it finally dawned on me that they were showing respect to me, a senior officer. During training, our instructors had told us that junior Marines would notice us and respond to our examples, but to have 65 guys stop dead in their tracks to pay respect to my rank when I was just casually walking past them was an eye-opening experience. The snap of their rifles and the sharpness of their salute jolted me into recognizing the responsibilities and privileges of my new position.

For most officers on Parris Island, receiving a show-stopping salute is a daily occurrence—nothing remarkable. But for me it was a defining moment. Marines were saluting me because of the bars on my collar, but I didn't feel worthy of that respect. However, the discomfort I felt at the respect they showed—respect that I knew I hadn't yet earned—inspired me to make sure I deserved that privilege. I was going to be the best officer I could be.

That day, I realized why Gunny Gerhart had worked so hard to spiff up my uniform. I was an example to the new recruits, who were being taught the importance of meeting and exceeding Marine Corps standards. Had I appeared in a "hosed up" uniform, as he called it, I would have sent a signal that just getting by was acceptable. And it isn't. I needed to demonstrate that I, too, was meeting and exceeding the standards, just as they were being asked to, and that the standards were the same no matter what your rank. That's what a leader does.

During our weeks together, the gunny also recounted stories of the best leaders he had ever worked for. He shared his role models with me, giving me a sense of the many ways I could lead from the front. There was Major Linton, who provided support for his troops whenever it was needed. And Captain Beckwith, who ran alongside his unit in formation runs even when he was not required to. "I didn't really get along with Captain Weston," Gunny admitted, "but he was always true to his word. If he made a commitment to help a Marine, or to look into something on behalf of one of his troops, everyone knew he would. He was tough, but his troops knew they could count on him." And there was General Swain. "He could have made things happen just by picking up the phone and barking an order," Gunny told me, "but he never did. He got things done by using his skills and abilities, not his connections. That really said a lot to his troops about the meaning of rank. Good leaders don't exploit their power." At my urging, and maybe a little badgering, Gunny Gerhart told story after story about the leaders he most admired. They weren't necessarily the most popular or the most fun-loving, but they were the leaders who truly exemplified leading from the front. They were the ones I wanted to be like.

With the gunny's guidance, I started to define for myself what kind of leader I wanted to be. I wanted to be respected, to set the example others looked to, to be the guiding force, charting the course. I wanted to bring the team together, inspiring them to follow me, not my rank. The leaders he talked about set the tone for their units, rallied them behind a mission, and were almost always successful in their tasks because they had the complete support of their troops. They had earned the gunny's respect. I wanted that respect, too.

Gunny Gerhart also told stories of officers who failed to meet Marine Corps standards and the impact that their failure had on their unit—generally low morale and a poor sense of camaraderie. He emphasized the importance of meeting physical fitness standards, warning me, "The fastest way to lose the respect of your troops is to fall out of a run or fail a PFT (physical fitness test)." And, being the leader that he is, while we were traveling, he made sure that I took time for physical therapy and low-impact workouts for my hip. He coached me and trained with me. He led me so that I could learn to lead others.

Although I was the officer in charge, he took control of the situation to help groom me to be a leader. He could have simply done his job as the videographer on the project, shot the video, and left, but he did much more. He lived leading from the front and, by example, helped me learn to live it, too.

Effective leadership in the Marine Corps meant supporting your troops so that your unit performed well, whether the task was an evaluation or a full-on assault on the enemy. Although the tasks are different in the corporate world, the value of leadership remains the same: assisting the organization in meeting its objectives, whether that means more new product introductions, increased sales, a better reputation, reduced expenses, or market share improvements. The better leader you are, the better your organization will perform and the greater the rewards you'll receive for your role.

> Learn, understand, and respect the unique performance standards of your organization. As a leader, you should continuously strive to meet and exceed those standards and to be a role model to those around you.

ENSURING THAT YOU MEET THE STANDARDS MEANS THAT YOU CAN PASS ANY TEST, ANY TIME

Angie

In the private sector, performance is often measured by sales records, customer satisfaction, or balanced budgets. In the Marine Corps, one of the most important performance criteria was physical fitness. Running with our coworkers was a regular occurrence, as was being tested on our fitness level.

I have always been a runner. From an early age, when I fell in love with road races, I have constantly pushed my body to perform. As a result, my leg muscles were well developed and strong. I could beat most women and many men in a running race, but I had no upper-body strength whatsoever. This was never a problem in high school, but being a fast runner was not enough to meet the full-body physical fitness standard set by the Marine Corps.

In college I was the only female midshipman who wanted to be a Marine. Despite my somewhat unusual position, the performance standard was the same. The Corps didn't care if I was a woman; I still needed to be able to run three miles, carry my own combat gear, and maintain a certain GPA to qualify. Although I had met ROTC's standards, Marine Corps officer training was beginning the summer between my junior and senior years in college, and if I couldn't hack the physical demands there, I'd be kicked out of ROTC. If that happened, I'd be sent a bill for the two years of tuition that ROTC had covered. I had a $25,000 incentive to pass every fitness test I encountered.

In preparation for officer training, I worked out religiously. I lifted weights, ran for miles, and learned how to do pull-ups—something that the Corps does not expect women to do. I passed the physical challenges of training with flying colors. I surprised myself by realizing that with the right amount of dedication and hard work, I could even exceed the standards the Corps asked of me.

I knew this mindset would serve me well in the Corps because, as a leader, I needed to be able to perform at the same level as my troops, if not better. In the Corps at least, it was unlikely that I'd have many women under my command—my troops would be almost all men. "I don't have to do that because I'm a girl" was a phrase I never wanted to utter. It would cost me the respect of my troops and damage my effectiveness as a leader. Meeting the standard was a way to gain the respect of my Marines, some of whom struggled more than I did. I resolved to train to be competitive with the men I would eventually lead, who I assumed would be much faster and stronger because of their build.

My training paid off three years later when, as part of my non-combat duties, I escorted 50 international officers around the Marine Corps base at Kaneohe Bay. (My mother used to boast to her friends that I was an escort, which they weren't initially sure was something to be proud of until she explained that I was a Marine Corps officer.) One of the stops on the tour, right after the rifle range and helicopter squadrons, was the obstacle course, where the group watched an all-male platoon complete the course. Impressed but curious, because I was the first female officer they had ever met, one officer asked: "Women don't do this, do they?" "Yes, they do," I told him.

"What about the rifles and the helicopters? Do women do those, too?" he asked. "Yes," I responded, which elicited some chuckles in the back of the group. Apparently, the idea of women serving alongside men on every task using the same equipment was a joke to them. They didn't believe that women like me were up to the task, which annoyed and offended me. What did I need to do to prove they were wrong, I wondered?

The international officers were under the impression that I was just window dressing for the Marine Corps. I wasn't surprised. I had experienced this reaction earlier in my career while serving in Puerto Rico alongside French Marines. As several platoons were getting ready to be transported in a five-ton vehicle, the French officers pulled me aside and told me to ride in the front seat. They were afraid I was too "delicate" to ride in the back. With a pack on my back, combat boots on my feet, and camouflage paint on my face, I certainly didn't feel "delicate," but I followed the order.

The visiting officers in Hawaii didn't quite believe that women met the same standards as men and challenged me to prove it. "Lieutenant, there's no way women can complete that obstacle course," one visitor told me. "Yes, they can, sir," I responded confidently. "No way," I heard from a few of the voices. "Prove it," someone shouted, which was followed by several supporting choruses of "Yeah, prove it!" Although frustrated by their skepticism, I was up for it. No problem.

I proceeded to run, jump, and climb my way through the difficult course with ease, just as I had done hundreds of times before. My irritation energized me. At the start, the officers looked on somewhat stunned, not quite believing what they were witnessing. But by the last obstacle, they were cheering me on. In their minds, I was breaking gender barriers. In my mind, it was just another day on the job. It was easy because I had been training regularly, following the men's regimen. I held myself to the same standard that the Marines under my command were expected to meet. I led from the front that day, but not by accident. As a leader, I knew that I wouldn't be challenged to meet the standards every day, but I needed to prepare every day in case I *was* challenged. You never know when you're going to be asked to be the example.

As one of the few women officers in the Marine Corps, I understood that my role was an important one. I had to be sure that I could meet the standard, or I would embarrass myself and damage the reputation of all women in the Corps. My inability to meet the standard would have suggested that other women in the Corps couldn't meet it, either. Fortunately, I had prepared, I was ready, and I succeeded.

Take the initiative and prepare before you are required to perform, whether that means knowing your department's financials inside and out, prepping for a new business presentation, or familiarizing yourself with your staff's career goals. Always be ready for the moment when you'll need to demonstrate your capabilities. Leaders are prepared.

DON'T ASK YOUR TEAM MEMBERS TO DO SOMETHING YOU AREN'T WILLING TO DO YOURSELF

Courtney

In the Marine Corps, the performance standards are clear and are the same for everyone in the Corps. A Marine's uniform and fitness level speak volumes about that individual's ability to perform. When I left the Corps for the private sector, I found that there were often two standards—one for managers and one for workers. This seemed odd and ineffective to me. I had been taught that leaders and followers should meet the same standards so that the whole organization could be more successful.

In the Corps, if your troops participated in an exercise, you, as their leader, were required to participate as well. That was the expectation, the standard. There was no picking and choosing which standards to uphold. But in the private sector, I saw that being a manager often meant that you didn't have to do anything you didn't want to. After leaving the Corps, I joined a software company as a sales manager. There, one of my least favorite tasks was "call marathons." In call marathons, which were held once a quarter, all sales representatives were required to make call after call to their customer list. Sometimes the challenge was to call 100 customers; other times there was a contest to see who could make the most calls in eight hours. It was an awful way to spend a day, but my boss was convinced that these phone-a-thons were an effective way to reach out to our customer base. Rewards for strong performance ranged from $100 gift certificates to dinners out. Such marathons may have achieved the company's goal of reaching out to customers, but the reps hated them. To be honest, so did I.

From the managers' perspective, call marathons weren't so bad. The managers were exempt from making calls, so they gathered in the conference room to work on other tasks, perhaps taking a long lunch on the company dime while the reps sweated it out on the phones. Since they had risen to the position of manager, they didn't have to dial phone numbers like their employees.

This double standard made me uncomfortable, but I went along with the routine during my first call marathon as a manager. I wasn't sure why I felt weird about it because call marathons had always been handled this way, I was told. But I felt bad about it nonetheless. As I watched my reps make call after tiring call, I wondered if sitting in the conference room was the best way to lead my employees. Was I doing all I could to support them? Was I comfortable sitting by while they made calls? I decided I wasn't.

The second call marathon rolled around a few months later, and I decided I didn't feel right about not pitching in. It seemed unfair of me to ask my team to do something that I wasn't willing to do myself. To lead from the front, I needed to be willing to make calls, too. And I did. That marathon, I sat with my sales team and made calls. What a difference! Seeing me there, working alongside them, my team increased its performance tenfold. I had participated mainly to make myself feel better about my role, but participating had the added benefit of energizing the reps. Bonus! I never sat out another one. Yes, I still hated making the calls as much as my team did—it was a boring way to spend the day. But as their leader, I couldn't ask them to give the effort their all if I wasn't willing to do so. It wasn't fair. My participation earned their respect, their loyalty, and their appreciation. In turn, they gave me, their leader, an even greater effort, which benefited us all.

 Look for opportunities to set an example. Tackle the tough projects or tasks that others shy away from to inspire others to do the same. And never allow your title or position to make you the exception to the rule—claiming an exemption is unfair and not leadership behavior.

EVERYDAY LEADERS

Leading from the front is about striving to be your best every day, holding yourself to the same standards to which you hold others, and being a role model to those around you, even those whom you don't know. Leaders aren't necessarily showy, but they do stand out.

Even if you haven't yet earned the official title of leader—manager, director, or partner, for example—you have the opportunity right now to start positioning yourself for that role. Don't wait for someone else to decide you're ready for the challenge—show those around you that you're already capable of it. You can do that in little ways. Taking the initiative to ask for new assignments, offering your assistance when you see that it might be needed, anticipating the needs of your boss (leaders don't wait to be told what to do because they're already doing it), and volunteering to train and mentor new employees are all ways you can demonstrate that you've earned the title. Until you've shown you're able to lead, you may not be given the title.

The old adage "Dress the part," or "Dress for the position you want to hold," is good advice. But fashion doesn't really affect promotion decisions—behavior does. Don't just dress the part; live the part. Striving to be a role model, a leader, will catch the eye of those around you. Set a positive example for your team members by being on time for meetings, for instance. Meet your deadlines as promised, rather than asking for an extension, and stay above the fray of office gossip. Leading isn't necessarily hard work, but it does require effort to be a role model.

But the role of a leader isn't limited to the workplace. Being a leader at home and in your community can be even more fulfilling. As a mom, you can lead your children by example. It's unreasonable to expect your children to behave in a calm, polite manner, for example, if you are rude and loud to them and to others. "Do as I say, not as I do" is perhaps least effective around children, who mimic what they hear and see. Your leadership can make their success easier and more profound.

You can also be a leader in your community and help make it better for everyone. Instead of being one of the neighborhood residents who point out problems but don't do anything about them, look for ways to initiate positive change. Maybe that means volunteering for the PTA, attending a city council meeting, or setting up a meeting with your school's principal. Leaders take action.

While leading from the front is your aspiration, you'll certainly have days when some areas of your life are particularly challenging—when it's a struggle to lead at all. We all have those days. Expecting yourself to be the perfect role model in all aspects of your life, 365 days a year, just isn't realistic. But making an effort to be a good role model is.

CHAPTER SUMMARY POINTS

- Leaders attempt to be good role models to anyone who is around them—you never know who is watching you for guidance on how to behave. Just as Marine Corps recruits watch officers for guidance on how to act and dress, people around you are watching you for leadership behavior, too. Set the standard by being the best you can.

- Leaders treat others with respect, take the initiative, and plan for the future. They're prepared. There's no way Angie could have completed the obstacle course successfully if she hadn't trained regularly to meet the Corps' performance standard. What standards does your organization have that you should be striving to meet or exceed? Continuing education credits? Certification? Performance targets? Make sure you're on course.

- Leaders hold themselves to the same high standards to which they hold others, rather than believing that they should be the exception to the rule. They don't ask others to do things they wouldn't do themselves. Courtney's decision to participate in her company's dreaded "call marathons" boosted her whole team's performance. Following the rules encourages others to do the same, which helps the whole team perform better.

- Leaders strive to be the best they can be, at every task, every day. Doing your best, no matter what the activity, improves your performance and inspires others to give the same amount of effort, which can have a major impact on the outcome. Take a look at how you run meetings, how you answer the phone, how quickly you respond to messages, how well you deal with crises—making a bigger effort to improve your performance on even small tasks can have a big impact on your job performance and on how you're perceived by those around you.

- Rank and title don't make someone a leader; behavior and attitude do. Anyone who is willing to invest the energy can be a leader. We were leaders in the Marine Corps, but not because of our officer status—the increased rank was the payoff for our hard work and performance. You can earn similar recognition by working hard to become a leader in all areas of your life.

CHAPTER 2

MAKE TIMELY DECISIONS—FIND THE 80 PERCENT SOLUTION

Leaders are decision makers. They're the ones who choose what their team will do next, as well as when, why, where, and how. They're comfortable making choices because they understand that decisions help the team make progress—the more decisions, the more resolution of issues, and the more issues resolved, the more success for those involved. At work, leaders choose how best to complete their missions—carry out their job duties, projects, or assignments—and how to support those around them. At home, leaders make the call regarding things like where to spend a week of vacation or what to do with a $2,000 tax refund. They take all the information at their disposal, consider what they know and what they think is best for their team or family, and make a decision.

Making decisions is exactly what a leader should do—it's what is expected of him or her. Leaders influence outcomes and inspire others. Followers, who may be team members, employees, children, parents, friends, or students, look to their leader for answers, for decisions. Every choice selected, every path chosen can move you toward a better situation. Granted, poor choices, such as deciding to start smoking again or deciding to spend money you don't have, can get you into trouble, but good decisions can help to correct poor ones, create opportunities, and make your life more enjoyable.

Yet many people we've encountered in our consulting work, especially women, express uncertainty about decision making—they don't trust their instincts when their choices affect others. We've heard from managers who like to avoid conflict and confrontation over decisions, and so put off making them. But procrastinating only heightens the managers' level of stress and may in fact reduce the quality of their choices. We've also seen people who are virtually paralyzed by the choices they have to make. They become stymied because they put too much emphasis on a single decision—way out of proportion to its importance—rather than viewing it as one in a series of decisions that have to be made. Avoiding making a decision generally leads to more frustration and uncertainty than making the decision quickly.

Take time management, for instance. To make the most effective use of your limited time, you need to make quick decisions about completing a task, taking a phone call, returning an e-mail, or participating in a meeting. Sorting through your commitments helps you prioritize and get more done, but you can't always say yes. Saying no to a new opportunity in order to meet the demands of a prior commitment will allow you to effectively manage one of your most precious resources, your time. In many circumstances, saying no can be a minor decision, but even minor decisions can have a big impact on your future.

We've noticed that many women have a hard time saying no, whether the decision is big or small. But when they don't say no, the implied response is yes, which can become a problem. An administrative assistant who attended our workshop (we'll call her Marcy) revealed that she found it difficult to say no to her colleagues. When her team members asked for her help in finishing their assignments, she never turned them down. But soon those in her section were routinely turning in incomplete reports, assuming that she would do the rest of their work for them. Instead of saying no and asking her team members to do their own work, Marcy had effectively chosen to continue doing the extra work for them.

High-impact decisions don't come up often, but when they do, you need to consider them carefully and then make the call. Deciding to pursue a new job with a higher salary but in a different city or to ask your current boss to match a competitor's job offer can yield great results. But these decisions need to be made in a timely manner or the opportunity may be lost.

Many times, the overriding concerns, fears, and anxieties that prevent us from making timely decisions are based on the mistaken belief that a decision has only two possible outcomes—a right one and a wrong one. Rarely is this the case. The results of a decision aren't always black or white, right or wrong. Often, the outcome is quite different from what you might have anticipated, especially if you are apprehensive about it. The only real negative from decision making is not making any decision at all. When you make a decision, you shape your future. When you allow circumstances or the opinions of others to influence your choices, you miss out on the chance to live your life the way you want to.

Certainly, there may be legitimate reasons for delaying or avoiding making a particular decision, but any delay diminishes the advantage of timeliness. One of the most common ways of delaying a decision is through information gathering or consensus building—a practice that women use much more than men. Instead of making an on-the-spot decision based on what they know, feel, or believe, some women consult a multitude of experts. They collect opinions from everyone—their girlfriends, friends, coworkers, mothers—before making a decision, even on something as trivial as where to take a client to lunch. Collecting various opinions and perspectives is valuable, but only in moderation. An additional opinion does not necessarily improve your decision-making capability or expand your list of options; it may only help to justify your having taken more time to make the call. So why waste the time? Go with your best assessment right off the bat and move on.

Most women want to make a perfect decision—one that everyone is happy with and that results in success—and this slows them down. Such a perfectionist goal is unrealistic—no decision is perfect, not everyone is going to like the choices you make, and not everyone is qualified to give you the best advice. Women have the ability to make informed decisions on their own. They just need to recognize that they will rarely have 100 percent of the information they need, and it's just not realistic to shoot for that.

Many women put so much pressure on themselves to make the "right" decision that they end up with a case of "analysis paralysis"—they get stuck. If they do make a decision, they often can't enjoy the benefits of being decisive because they second-guess themselves, wondering whether they made the right call or should have considered other options. We all know women who probably lie awake at night replaying and almost obsessing over a decision they have already made. This unhealthy focus on a past decision puts them in danger of missing out on new opportunities. Leaders make decisions based on the information they have, then move ahead to the next decision. They don't look back.

The Marine Corps uses 80 percent information as the target, acknowledging that you're never going to have all the information you need to make a perfect decision. Also, having all the information is frequently not necessary. You generally know which decision is right for you with far less than 100 percent information. Let's say you've been given your choice of assignments at work: one where you'll work closely with your new boss, or another where you'll have less contact but more control over the end result. You probably have an immediate gut feeling as to which would be better for your career (and there's no right answer in this case). Sure, you can talk with your colleagues, with HR, with a career coach, and with anyone else who'll listen, but you'll never be absolutely certain you're making the right choice. And that's OK—just go with your instincts.

By making decisions about issues you can control, you achieve progress—you influence outcomes, rather than remaining stuck. You also become better prepared to recognize and respond to new opportunities and challenges that come up. Timely decisions are proactive; they help you move forward. Procrastinating only puts you in a reactive mode in which you give up opportunities to lead your life.

A GOOD DECISION TODAY IS BETTER THAN
A GREAT DECISION TOMORROW

Angie

Making the decision to join the Marines proved that even at a young age, Courtney and I could make the tough calls. However, during Officer Candidate School, our decision-making abilities were kicked up a notch through repeated skill-building exercises. At the time, we thought we were learning how to lead infantry attacks. But really, we were being taught the fundamentals of a good decision.

In my fifth week of Officer Candidate School, my platoon was warned that we had a big day ahead of us the next day. We weren't sure exactly what that meant, but we hit the sack at 10:00 p.m. to rest up for the exercise. Two hours later, the bright lights in the barracks suddenly came on, and I heard our three sergeant instructors barking orders: "Wake up! Wake up! Get out of your racks, grab your gear, and get outside in formation," they yelled at the top of their lungs. I scrambled out of bed mechanically. During the next five minutes, the 49 other members of my platoon and I flailed about, confused and dazed. We threw on our uniforms; tied our boots; grabbed our helmets, packs, and rifles; and moved outside. We lined up for a march that led us about 10 miles into the woods.

Once we arrived at base camp, we set up our tents in the dark, arranged our gear, and by 4 a.m. were eating breakfast—those tasty MREs, meals-ready-to-eat. I was hoping for an omelet with ham, my favorite prepackaged meal, but instead I got the "five fingers of death"—hot dog links, my least favorite. I'd had two hours of sleep and had marched 10 miles, and now I was eating hot dogs at the crack of dawn. I thought I'd hit a new low. But, of course, this was just the beginning of the day—there were many more low periods to come.

That morning we were told we would be tested on small-unit leadership. For the first event, we organized ourselves into groups of four, called "fire teams" (the smallest unit in the Marine Corps), and took turns leading each other in attacks against an enemy group. Once we completed an attack, we ran three miles to a 15-minute Reaction Course designed to test our ability to lead small units through realistic wartime scenarios.

The Reaction Course itself was a series of 10- by 20-foot chain-link-fenced cages, with high interior walls to prevent us from seeing inside the other cages. Within each cage were obstacles that related to a particular scenario we might face in wartime, such as traversing a rushing river, removing an injured comrade from the battlefield, or safely conducting a resupply of allied forces. The cages were filled with man-made structures designed to imitate elements you would find in the field. It was up to the fire team leader to solve the problem at hand.

Once that was done, we ran three miles back to do another small-unit attack, which was followed by another run and another Reaction Course problem. It was early August, when the temperature was near 90 degrees at dawn and would rise past 100 by noon. Our feet were still blistered and swollen from the previous day, and we were running in combat boots and full gear. We were exhausted from the workout, yet the Corps expected us to function as warriors. Barely conscious, I wasn't sure I could do it. But at this point, I had no other option. I had to give this event my best.

Each member of the fire team had to lead one attack and one Reaction Course problem, which meant that over the next few hours, we ran more than 20 miles in combat gear with only short breaks to contemplate life-and-death situations.

I was the second person in my fire team to lead a small-unit attack and Reaction Course problem. When my turn came to lead the attack, I approached the captain to hear my scenario. He told me that there was an enemy bunker that my fire team had to attack. He gave me a map with the grid coordinates for our location and the grid coordinates for the bunker on it, but little else in the way of information. I had to decide how to approach the bunker and whether we should stay close together or spread out, then use my land navigation skills to get us there.

I nervously briefed my fire team while the captain stood by, evaluating me. This was all new to me, and I hoped that my training would result in combat victory, especially since I was being graded. I was very aware of the captain's presence as I explained to the team our orientation, our mission, how we were going to execute the attack, and how we would communicate with each other and our senior command. Then we headed out toward our objective.

We were deep in the woods, where there were few landmarks to help us keep track of where we'd been and where we were going as we moved stealthily toward our enemy target, which was about one-half mile away. I needed to keep my team together, but not too close, or the enemy could potentially kill us all with one live grenade or easily round us up as prisoners. Our faces were painted in camouflage, to blend in with our surroundings, but a side effect was that it was harder to pick out my team as we moved silently toward our objective. I needed to communicate to keep my unit together and moving in concert, but I wasn't allowed to speak at all—only hand and arm signals were permitted.

Small-unit attacks really test the leader's decision-making skills. You can't talk with your team members, though you're supposed to be guiding them toward your common objective, and you never know when the enemy (other Marines role-playing to make the exercise more realistic) will attack you. Only after the enemy fires at you can you begin talking to your unit and fighting back. Quickly giving orders is key to mounting a successful assault and saving the lives of your team—hesitating is deadly, and consensus building is not an option. You have to make the call yourself.

Keeping all this in mind, I led the team toward what I believed was the location of the bunker. Unfortunately, we missed it by 25 yards and were counterattacked by enemy forces. My team suffered casualties as a result of my leadership, and I was devastated. I had done my best, but apparently many of my decisions during the attack had been wrong. I was extremely frustrated. How could I be a leader if my judgment didn't result in battlefield victory?

My only hope of passing the test was to hear if my instructor, the captain, had a different interpretation of the attack he had just witnessed. I approached him to learn what I had done right and what I had done wrong. He had a lot to say about the latter. After he was finished, I boldly asked him if I had passed the test. He looked at me like I was an idiot. He then deadpanned, "Candidate, half your team is dead—what do you think?" I felt ridiculous for having asked the question. Obviously, I must have failed if half my team was dead, right? The captain wasn't giving any answers.

But I didn't have time to dwell upon my stupid question because it was my turn to lead my team on the three-mile run and Reaction Course problem. Outside, I was briefed on the scenario my team was about to encounter inside the cage. Armed with a piece of rope, three boards, and a barrel, we had 15 minutes to rescue a POW on the other side of a raging river. The clock started as soon as we entered the cage, where I expected to see an actual whitewater river and a bound and gagged Marine (hey, they were impressive when it came to setting up real-life scenarios, and I expected this to be just another example). What I found instead, however, was a plastic-lined 8- by 5-foot box filled with water (the "river") and a stuffed, 100-pound dummy on the other side. It looked pretty easy at first, until I realized I was expected to play along with the scenario, acting like a leader facing a harrowing situation. I got into character. As I was plotting my strategy down in the cage, above me on catwalks were officers watching my every move, grading my approach and response. It was nerve-wracking. I tried to ignore them and focus on the task.

"Candidate Jeffries," I instructed, "grab the barrel and use it to float to the other side of the river." Whoops, Jeffries rolled over in the box and fell in the water; he was "dead" and had to sit out the rest of the exercise. That decision changed the scenario again; now I had only two teammates to help me rescue the POW. The minutes slipped away as I worked through Plan B.

"Candidate Michaels, grab the rope and let's tie the ladder in place to get across the river," I ordered. The ladder was too rickety. Michaels fell in the water, and one of the instructors pronounced him dead. I was getting frustrated and wished it was an actual raging river—it might have been easier to cross. Just as I was about to act on my Plan C, the game was over; time was up.

All the Reaction Course problems turned out to be similar. The challenge was acting quickly and decisively with limited information. There was no time to gather ideas from my troops or to take a vote; it was up to me as the leader. I was graded on how quickly I began making decisions after hearing the scenario and how much time elapsed before I briefed my squad. During those 15 minutes, I was constantly making choices and course corrections based on new factors, such as a teammate dying or defective equipment. Once again, my squad failed the task. I left the exercise feeling like a loser. How was I ever going to be a leader if my decisions always resulted in disaster, I wondered to myself.

When I received my official grades for the exercise, I was shocked to see that I had decent scores on both the small-unit attack and the Reaction Course. Puzzled, I asked my officer-in-charge, Captain Anderson, how I could fail the attack and Reaction Course problem and still pass. She explained that the Corps didn't expect me to lead a perfect attack; I was being graded on my ability to make decisions. This was news to me—the Marine Corps thrived on precision, and I assumed that being "perfect" was part of that equation. But as I listened to her, I heard her explain that the grading officers had judged me on my ability to lead my team under intense circumstances and to keep forcing action, rather than being indecisive. By making decisions quickly, I controlled the situation to a greater degree. She reassured me that the Corps would help me improve my land navigation skills later, to help me become more precise in locating the enemy, and that I'd have more practice with leading small units. It turns out that the Reaction Course problems are rarely solvable, but my willingness to continue making decisions about the next course of action was a sign that I had raw leadership skills. The Corps could hone my decision-making abilities as it made me a stronger leader.

> Good decisions can be made with limited information, and perfect decisions are unrealistic. Practice making timely decisions when the stakes are low, and by the time you have to make a tough call, you'll be prepared to handle the pressure and make a decision quickly.

PROCRASTINATION ONLY PROLONGS THE PROBLEM

Angie

The Marine Corps developed my decision-making skills for the battlefield, and it expected me to apply the same abilities to leading people. During one of my first assignments leading troops, I learned a
critical lesson about the importance of timeliness in decision making.

Nearly every Marine struggles when he or she first enters the
Corps, so when I saw that one of my troops in Hawaii was having
difficulty adjusting, I wasn't overly concerned. Yes, Private First Class
(PFC) Andrew Schroeder was showing up late for scheduled physical training, which was a serious offense, and his uniform looked
disheveled and his boots scuffed, but I figured he just needed a little more time to catch on to the Marine Corps way of life. Sure, his
work wasn't quite up to par, but I didn't want to ruin his career by
ordering official counseling or punishment. That seemed heavy-
handed at this stage of the game. So I decided to wait it out, hoping
that he'd pull himself together on his own.

That day never came. Several weeks later, after one of Schroeder's
infamous "no-shows," my gunny, Gunnery Sergeant Ryan Ellis,
stopped by my office so that we could chat.

"What's up, Gunny?" I asked. I could tell there was something
on his mind.

"Ma'am, we've been getting some calls about PFC Schroeder
from collection agencies," he told me. "He's overdue on a bunch of
bills, apparently. He also hasn't been completing assigned projects,
and he failed his physical fitness test."

"You're kidding me, right? I can't believe he's gotten himself into
more trouble," I sighed.

"What do you mean? Has he done something else?" he asked.

"Well, where should I begin? He's been oversleeping, arriving at
training late . . ."—before I could finish, I saw Gunny's facial expres-
sion change from confusion to concern.

"Ma'am, why didn't you tell me about this sooner?" he asked.

"I knew he was having a tough time adjusting, and I wanted to give him a chance to shape up," I admitted.

"Ma'am, I've been in the Corps for 18 years, and I've seen plenty of Marines screw up. But this is beyond screw-ups," said Gunny Ellis. "The second time he overslept should've been a warning sign that this Marine was in trouble."

He was right. I'd known instinctively that Schroeder wouldn't be able to pull himself out of his downward spiral, but I didn't yet trust myself to take action. Talking to Gunny, it was clear to both of us that when I first started noticing problems, I'd had enough information to act. By waiting, I had prolonged the situation, allowing the problems to continue and worsen.

It was now time for me to show Gunny, and myself, that I had what it took to be the decisive leader that the Marine Corps wanted me to be. I needed to make some unpopular, but smart, decisions as far as Schroeder was concerned. Gunny helped me develop a disciplinary plan of action to help PFC Schroeder get back on track. I knew Schroeder wasn't going to like what I had to tell him, but he faced barracks restriction and a hold on his promotion to lance corporal if he didn't shape up. I reminded myself that although I couldn't make the right decisions for him, I could provide guidance to help influence his decisions in the future.

Gunny tried to make me feel better about my actions, telling me: "Ma'am, 90 percent of your time will be spent on 10 percent of your Marines. Be aware of it, so that you can more quickly identify which 10 percent need that extra guidance."

I recognized that had I been decisive and taken action regarding his poor performance weeks ago, Schroeder might not be in as much trouble now. That *was* my fault. Decisions that affect other people are often the hardest to make, but they are also the ones where time is of the essence. Waiting and hoping that the situation would resolve itself was not leadership behavior, and I knew it.

But I also knew that my actions were stereotypically female. In general, women are raised to be consensus builders and peacemakers, not conflict makers. We're expected to help keep situations harmonious, rather than taking steps that may cause conflict and discomfort. And that was what PFC Schroeder was facing—conflict and discomfort. Fortunately, my gunny helped me recognize that the conflict was Schroeder's doing, not mine, and that, as a leader, it was my responsibility to try and bring him back in line. He also reminded me that while my peacemaking efforts were often valuable, they weren't productive when they caused me to be indecisive.

I had waited to be 100 percent sure that PFC Schroeder really needed formal guidance, although I was at least 80 percent sure to begin with. I shouldn't have procrastinated on a decision when I already had enough information to make an informed, timely call. My hesitation only gave Schroeder the opportunity to get into more trouble, forcing me into reactive mode. I wish I had been more proactive early on in helping Schroeder make the transition from civilian to Marine. That would have saved us both a lot of heartache.

Delaying making a decision wastes valuable energy and slows down progress. Procrastination also allows small problems to become larger ones. A better tactic is to make a decision quickly, even if it's based on instinct alone.

TRUST YOUR GUT WHEN IT'S DECISION TIME

Courtney

Just as Angie struggled at first with making decisions that affected others, I struggled with decisions about my own life. After leaving active duty and heading out into the "real" world, I had a pretty clear idea of what kind of career I wanted. Yet somehow I got sidetracked by all the choices in front of me.

I attended law school using the G.I. Bill, but I never really intended to practice after graduating. I thought my degree might be a useful credential down the road, and my time in the business world had reinforced that perception. I enjoyed studying law and had done well at William and Mary, but I had my heart set on owning my own business after graduation, not joining a law firm. Then I received information from the campus recruitment office that highlighted a variety of legal careers.

The William and Mary career placement office does an excellent job of finding positions for its graduates. Each year hundreds of prestigious law firms arrive on campus to interview potential job candidates at the school, all organized by the career placement pros; my year was no different.

The career counselor encouraged me to participate in the campus recruiting process. "Why not see what's out there?" he suggested. I had long ago decided that I wasn't interested in a legal job, but when the opportunities were right in front of me, I caved in to curiosity. "What the heck," I thought. "It might be fun to see what kinds of jobs are out there." I thought I had a clear career plan, but I wavered when other opportunities were presented to me. That was my first mistake.

Before entering law school, I had carefully mapped out my career and considered my goals. Most important were quality of life, a job that required creativity and provided variety, a chance to build my own company, and a position where I could also balance a family. I didn't want to be a small player in a massive law firm, handling the same kinds of cases day after day. I wanted to be challenged, but I also wanted to be constantly learning and doing different things. I was very clear about what I wanted, until the lure of big money sucked me in.

I'm a competitive person, and no matter what I'm attempting, I want to do well. I guess the legal recruiters saw that trait in me and liked it. Soon I was getting callback interviews at hiring law firms, where I would fly to their office at their expense, enjoy a nice hotel stay and maybe a little room service, and then fly back to school. The offers started coming in—really big offers. I was astounded at the amount of money I could make. I hadn't realized what I'd be giving up by starting my own company right out of law school. I started imagining what that money could do for me—a house, vacations, less worry about bills.

I must admit, I got caught off guard by the possibility of instant wealth. It appealed to me, that's for sure! My law school friends were impressed by the firms that were pursuing me, and this made me reconsider my plan to start my own business immediately. With all that money being offered, maybe I could work for a year, earn enough money to fund my business, and then leave. That sounded like a logical plan, I rationalized.

In truth, I was second-guessing the decision I had made earlier about the kind of life I wanted to lead. Also, I was delaying taking a risk. It might have looked as if I was taking the bull by the horns, but I was really procrastinating like a pro. Rather than making decisions about how to start my new business, I was focusing my energy on landing a job I didn't even want. My indecisiveness continued, and I accepted a job that took me away from what I really wanted— my own business.

I accepted an internship with a prestigious law firm on the East Coast, to the cheers and hugs of my classmates. I wasn't nearly as excited as they were, but the money was good. It was to be a three-month trial period, during which the law firm could size me up for a permanent position and I could decide if it was where I wanted to be.

During those three months, I reflected on my initial career plan. I began to realize that my indecisiveness where my career was concerned was costing me time and energy. My colleagues at the law firm were interesting, the practice was thriving, and the money was amazing, but something wasn't right. The work itself was not fulfilling to me. Rather than interacting regularly with coworkers in the office, I spent most of my time squirreled away in a room by myself researching cases. It didn't play to my strengths, that's for sure. I tried to ignore the feeling in the pit of my stomach and instead worked to convince myself that this was a great place to be. Everyone around me was telling me how lucky I was to be working there. But I knew it had been a mistake.

I turned to a friend to sort out what was going on in my career, and whether I was where I should be. She cut right to the chase with just a few questions: "What is this law firm doing to help you own your own business? That's what you really want, isn't it?" she asked.

Yes, that was what I really wanted. And, truthfully, my current job was moving me further away from what I wanted, not closer to it. But the money was hard to walk away from, I tried to explain.

"You'll make money anywhere, Courtney. How is this job developing your skills? What else are you getting from this experience?" she wanted to know. And I had no answers. It was clear that the job was not right for me. I had been lured away from my original career plan, and I needed to correct the situation right away. I needed to be decisive.

At the end of the three-month internship, I was given a formal offer of full-time employment. I thanked my boss profusely and promptly rejected it. "No" was the right answer for me, although it took some convincing to get the law firm to see it my way. The practice group manager called me into his office that day and asked that I put off making a decision until the end of the year (essentially delaying my rejection), by which time I'd have a better sense of the firm. He worked hard to persuade me to stay, to reconsider, but I stood fast in my decision. I explained that my internship had been useful, but that I knew I was meant for self-employment and wanted to get to work on building my business. Staying there wouldn't help me achieve that. Eventually he relented. He told me I was the first person in a while to turn them down.

My law school friends were mystified: "You're crazy to turn that down!" "What are you thinking?!" "Now what are you going to do?" What I was going to do was start my own business—my plan all along. I wasn't exactly sure how I was going to do this, but I knew it was what I truly wanted. I had 80 percent of the information—Angie and I were working on outlining a book we wanted to write (this one), we had just landed an agent, and we had a business concept to develop. The remaining 20 percent of the information (my instincts and experience) confirmed that I would be happy only if I was working on my own business right now. I had all the information I needed.

I had been indecisive at first, when I spent valuable time interviewing for jobs and getting caught up in the excitement of the process. That indecision had gotten me into trouble, pulling me into a legal job I didn't want. But once I realized my mistake, I resolved to correct it immediately. And I did.

The happy ending to the story is that Angie and I founded Lead Star in 2004, which has quickly grown into a thriving leadership consulting firm. Had I stayed with the law firm, I would never have had the opportunity to shape my own career and start a business we both love.

When I look back at some of the setbacks in my life, I see a pattern of indecision. In some cases, I couldn't decide fast enough, so I missed out on things, like vacation trips with friends or time with loved ones. In others, I couldn't decide at all, so I just went with the flow, as with my job at the law firm. Saying yes was easier. At each point in the process, I should have said no. I really should have said no after the first round of interviews. And I could have said no when I was offered the internship, but I didn't. I wasn't ready to make the tough choice. Instead, I let myself be swayed by what my friends thought or by what I thought society expected of me, and so ended up with a poor choice—because I hadn't made it. I wasn't leading my life; I was letting other people's opinions and preferences lead me.

Saying no to opportunities can be difficult and unpopular, but often it's the choice you must make in order to do what's right for you. Turning down opportunities can also allow better ones to present themselves.

LEADING IN TIMES OF UNCERTAINTY

We hear frequently that we currently live in a time of uncertainty, as if there had previously been a time when we knew exactly what to expect every minute of our lives. If only! Truthfully, every day is uncertain, and that's what makes it such an opportunity. Every day is an opportunity for you to take another step toward the life you want to lead. Every choice, every decision you make can get you closer to the balance you need, the career success you seek, the fulfillment you've been looking for, no matter what your goal is. Putting off decisions or letting others make your decisions for you is not leadership behavior. Instead, you are allowing society and circumstances to influence what happens in your life.

You can quickly take charge of your life by making your own decisions and taking the initiative. Your choices and actions set you apart from the crowd—ahead of the crowd, where you can serve as a role model for those around you. Deciding today that you will lead your own life will inspire others to do the same.

CHAPTER SUMMARY POINTS

- In order to lead the life you want, you need to make decisions. Avoiding decisions means that you've handed off decision-making power to others. That is, others are controlling *your* future. Work to make decisions as soon as they arise instead of obsessing over them, as Angie learned to do in the Reaction Course training. Make them and move on to your next exciting choice.

- Decision making can be stressful. Recognize that you will rarely have 100 percent of the information you need to make a perfect choice. The tough calls you have to make in life are challenging because you have limited information and can't predict the future. By making the choice you think is best for you, you're increasing the odds of your ultimate success. The alternative, making no choice or decision at all, is surely worse than anything you could have chosen. Making a decision will get you one step closer to your objective.

- Procrastination is a choice all on its own. It takes time, energy, and resources to procrastinate, and you get none of the benefits of progress, as Angie learned when she chose to ignore PFC Schroeder's problems, which only made the situation worse. By taking no action at all, you may pass up important, valuable opportunities. Instead of postponing a decision, resolve to make one soon after the choice arises. The bigger the choice, the more time you should take to decide—but, in general, you shouldn't ever need more than a few days. If you need more than that, you're probably procrastinating, which is not leadership behavior.

- When you are stuck on a choice—from a major life decision to what outfit to wear—push yourself to make the call solely with the information you have now. If Courtney had turned down

51

the chance to interview for law firm positions up front, as her gut was telling her to, she could have avoided months of wasted time and energy interviewing for jobs she knew she didn't want. Instead of delaying, she should have made a decision. Don't put off making a decision—make it now, with the information you have on hand. With practice, making timely decisions will become a natural habit, and your confidence as a leader will be strengthened.

CHAPTER 3

SEEK TO TAKE RESPONSIBILITY BEFORE YOU BEGIN TO PLACE BLAME

People don't become leaders by staying beneath the radar and avoiding responsibility—they earn their position at the front of the pack by doing the exact opposite: taking responsibility. They aren't afraid to say, "It was my fault," if a problem was their doing, or even to bear the brunt of criticism in order to protect their team from the same treatment. Leaders are out in front, serving as role models, and are willing to assume responsibility for every success or failure that comes their way.

Leaders recognize that accepting responsibility for their actions and inactions is the first step in achieving success, but many of the people we speak to, especially women, are still striving to find the right balance when it comes to employing this principle. Some cling to the notion that they must always look perfect in the eyes of others and should distance themselves from mistakes, even when something was truly their fault, while others accept too much responsibility. Placing blame on others or on circumstances only impedes progress.

Leaders want results and aren't afraid to acknowledge their own role in a problem in order to bring about resolution. For many women, it's easier to blame someone or something else for when life feels out of control rather than to consider how we may be causing our own problems. "It's my husband's fault for not helping out more" or "It's my boss's fault for piling on more work than one person can do," we've heard women in our audiences say. "I have no time to work out. Between work and my family, I've got nothing left." It takes little effort to shift blame from ourselves to anything we can find: poor technology, too much food, too little money, other people—you name it. The list goes on and on and on. It's someone else's doing, someone else's responsibility.

Many of us work harder and harder in an attempt to gain control, and when that doesn't produce the desired result, we assume that something or someone else must be interfering. It's their fault, not mine, we may think, because I'm doing all I can. Unfortunately, this approach to problem solving doesn't help us make progress. Effort doesn't always equate to progress.

The Marines taught us that simply trying harder isn't enough. When a commanding officer issues an order, you either succeed or fail in the mission—there's no "almost." And if you fail, the commander isn't interested in hearing excuses and finger pointing. When you botch a mission and get your Marines killed, it's not enough to say "I tried," or "the radio didn't work, and I didn't know what to do." We learned that we were responsible for the mission—succeed or fail. Excuses don't save lives.

This "no excuses" mindset taught us to look internally (not externally) first when we weren't successful. When we faced an obstacle, we learned to identify the problem, examine our actions, implement a new course, and get on with it. Excuses got us nowhere. Many women haven't yet figured that out, and it's holding them back from leading more satisfying lives.

Take the issue of equal pay, for example. Women we speak to often complain that they are paid less than their male colleagues, and they blame their employer. Yet when we ask about their last round of salary negotiations, we frequently hear that there were none: the company offered a certain salary, and the women were so excited to be selected for the promotion or offered the new job that they just accepted what was presented. Instead of asking for more money, as the company is presumably expecting, women are much more likely than men to take the first offer made. When women accept responsibility for how much money they make, they're often more proactive in negotiations—they're more comfortable asking for more because they know they're worth it. Leaders look at inequities, such as pay gaps, with an eye toward what they could have done differently to change the outcome.

The key to achieving your goals and living a life that is in balance begins with taking responsibility for your actions and your decisions, rather than making excuses for your shortcomings. When you own your life, you will be much more fulfilled. You'll have more time for family, accomplish more at work with less effort, experience greater satisfaction in relationships, get promoted, lose weight, or whatever you strive for. By taking responsibility, examining your actions, and implementing new ones (just as we learned to do in the Marines), you can achieve your goals and lead your life.

ACCEPTING RESPONSIBILITY IS THE FIRST STEP TOWARD SUCCESS

Courtney

I learned the Marine Corps' way of taking responsibility soon after becoming an officer. About 2½ months into officer training, I came up against the Marine Corps' Endurance Course. If I passed the test, I'd finish my training on time and move on to serve in the Fleet Marine Force. If I failed, I'd join "Mike" Company, a group of new officers waiting to be recycled into a new six-month training cycle; my career would be in limbo.

Although having to join Mike Company would be embarrassing, it was failure that really scared me. Until then, I had never failed at anything significant. Sure, I'd had slip-ups in my teen years. But this time, I had a lot more at stake.

And there was something worse than the threat of Mike Company. Only days before, I had enrolled my mother in a special medical program for Marine Corps relatives that would provide the diagnostic tests and chemotherapy to treat her rare type of blood cancer. If I couldn't pass the Endurance Course, I could be deemed "unfit for service," and if that happened, my mother would lose this life-saving medical treatment at Bethesda Naval Hospital. I feared the Endurance Course because I had officially failed to pass it twice already. I had one more chance to pass, for my sake and my mother's.

The obstacles in the Endurance Course are set up in a space about the length of a football field and wide enough for four Marines to maneuver at a time. To pass the first part, you have four minutes to climb over an eight-foot metal bar, sprint and jump over a seven-foot wooden plank wall, climb over a series of five-foot-tall wooden logs, shimmy down elevated metal bars, descend a group of vertical logs, and, finally, climb up 25 feet of rope.

I couldn't climb the rope.

By the time I made it to the rope, my arms ached from the beating I'd just given them, and I was sweating profusely. I'd make it up six feet and then freeze. My arms couldn't carry me. I was embarrassed, frustrated, and depressed as I watched the rest of my squad scale the rope with ease. And, to make matters worse, after failing the rope climb, I still had to continue with the second part of the course, a grueling five-mile run through hilly, wooded terrain.

For the next 40 minutes or so, as I ran, I would replay in my mind my failure to climb the rope. How could I climb up 25 feet of rope in 60 seconds? I had never climbed a rope before. Who were they kidding? I'm 5'8" and weigh 135 pounds. I don't have the upper body strength a man does and never will. So why was I expected to meet the same training requirements? It was unfair. And watching the men fly up the rope in seconds only made me angrier. Of course they could do it; they were a lot stronger.

I'd met every challenge the Marine Corps had posed so far. I marched several miles in full combat gear every day. I'd qualified at the rifle range on both the pistol and the rifle. I'd passed the swim test, treading water for 10 minutes, making a flotation device out of my pants, and swimming 500 meters. Despite never having camped out before, I'd survived squad-a-thons during which we spent two nights outdoors learning squad infantry tactics. I had been successful on every other test—why couldn't I do this?

After my second "E" course failure, Captain Adams summoned me to her office. She stood 5'4", with a strong, muscular build and impressive guns that protruded from under her short-sleeved shirt. Her mission was to weed out women who couldn't meet Marine Corps standards for physical performance—me included.

As she started to rant and rave about how I was on the "fast track to nowhere" because I couldn't climb "one little short rope," I agreed with her. I knew that only 25 feet of rope stood between me and success, but it might as well have been 25,000 feet—that's how insurmountable it seemed. Standing there in Captain Adams's office, I had hit rock bottom.

She raged on about how I was an embarrassment to the Corps, and I began having a silent conversation with her in my head. "Yep, I'm a failure. Yep, I know I suck," I responded mentally. In the military you are never permitted to be disrespectful by talking back to a senior officer, so I coped by having a dialogue with her in my head. She continued to shout at me, and I continued to agree, albeit in my head, "If you don't pass, you'll be out of the Corps in no time, Lieutenant," she continued. A transfer to Mike Company was a slippery slope to discharge, she warned.

Her threat hit me like a slap in the face, shocking me into reality. If I couldn't climb the rope, my mother would lose her medical care. I'd lose my paycheck, and the Corps could ultimately force me out for underperformance. The only way to guarantee a continued spot in the Corps is to continue to perform, to be promoted, and to move up the hierarchy. If I failed, I was headed down and out.

Slowly I began to hear a defiant voice in my head. "You're a disgrace to women in the Marine Corps," said Captain Adams, but the voice in my head responded boldly, "No, I'm not. I'm trying hard!" "You must do better or you'll be dropped from this company," she boomed. "I fought hard to be a Marine, and I'm not giving up over a damn rope," I shouted back inside. My inner voice was picking up steam. "Besides, my mom needs me. If I get kicked out of the Corps, she'll have no medical care. I know I can do this. I can climb a rope!" I told myself. "I've just got to dig deeper."

As the dialogue in my head continued, I found an inner strength, and inner confidence that told me I could do it; I just needed to find a new approach.

I finally realized what I'd been doing. In my despair and frustration, I had assumed that my energy and effort would somehow make it work. And when my effort, my endless "trying" didn't pay off, I stopped taking responsibility for my actions and wallowed in excuses. I blamed others—the Marine Corps, my colleagues, my instructors, my gender, even the rope itself—and concluded that it just wasn't fair. What I really needed to do instead was to focus on me and what I could do to get myself up that rope. I had never bothered to own the problem and ask, "Am I doing this right? Is there a better way?" Now I knew the truth. The Corps had shown me that I was the only person responsible for my poor performance on the rope.

After my meeting, I headed back to the barracks, determined to find a way to pass the test. One of my roommates, Emily Watson, was already there. "I have to find a way to climb that rope," I told her. Emily could climb the rope easily, a fact that I had dismissed as a fluke. Though I hated to admit it, most women could climb the rope. Angie had no problem making it up and down the rope in a little less than a minute.

"Let me help you," Emily offered. She then shared a critical piece of information: "It's not your arm strength, it's your feet. You need to get a good hold on the rope with your feet, then push yourself up instead of pulling." That evening and the next, after completing a long day's work, which included practice runs of the endurance course, we came back to the barracks, grabbed our car keys, and drove back to the course. We pointed the cars toward the rope climb and turned on the high beams to illuminate the area. With Emily's guidance, I pushed off and up. That first night, I made it halfway up the rope. By the next night, I could make it to the top. And on my final chance to pass the endurance course, I made it. My time: 3 minutes and 52 seconds.

Though it had taken several weeks, I learned a lesson that I'll never forget. When I'm faced with an obstacle—whether it's a 25-foot rope, too much work, or those last 10 pounds I can't seem to lose—I don't need to look far for a solution. I need to look within myself for a successful approach. I learned to not be blinded by the effort and energy I put into a task, but to own the problem, identify the challenges, and implement change. The Corps taught me that taking responsibility involves assessing your weaknesses, developing a solution to overcome them, and taking action.

Blaming others or circumstances beyond your control gets you nowhere. You can't make progress until you take responsibility. Working to identify what you could have done differently—where you can make a change—moves you closer to a solution, to success.

While I learned about accepting responsibility from the endurance course, Angie learned about responsibility the Marine Corps way when she assumed leadership of her base's newspaper. This was her first chance to prove herself as a successful leader, and it all came down to accepting responsibility.

TAKE RESPONSIBILITY FOR FAILURE IN ORDER TO GENERATE SOLUTIONS

Angie

As a second lieutenant public affairs officer (PAO) at Marine Corps Base Hawaii in Kaneohe, one of my jobs was to plan stories for, copy edit, and lay out *The Hawaii Marine*, the weekly base newspaper. This wasn't the adventurous job I had envisioned when I joined the Marine Corps, but it was highly visible, so I couldn't blow it off.

On my second week on the job, I was totally overwhelmed. I had five full-time combat correspondents doing the work of eight, and all of them, like me, were new to the job. It was July, when Marines rotate into new positions, and my team had just begun its new assignment. We were all inexperienced and facing an impending deadline. Few of my Marines had experience writing newspaper stories, some of the stories that had been written for the current issue had not been approved and had to be rewritten, our graphic design guru was still in training, and we were running behind schedule.

Generals use base papers to communicate with their Marines, reporting on significant accomplishments, honors, news, and events.

Having an issue printed late would reflect poorly on my general and his leadership—a situation I didn't want. I was going to do anything to avoid a late newspaper.

The night before our due date, I kept the combat correspondents until after midnight to finish the job. Marines usually go home at 5:00 p.m. so that they can get to the chow hall in time for dinner, so this was unusual, and they weren't happy. Like me, they were frustrated and tired, but the worry-induced adrenaline kept us functioning. We couldn't stomach telling the general that we had let him down and that this week's paper wouldn't be out on time.

Part of the problem was that the people on my staff were trained to write stories and take photos in the field but weren't skilled at layout and production. Neither was I, for that matter. Still, we managed to complete the stories, process the photos, get them in place, and deliver the issue to the printer in time for printing and distribution the next day. The product we produced was legible, but certainly would never have been in the running for a Pulitzer Prize. We left our shop in the dark, exhausted.

I vowed never to go through that miserable experience again.

On my drive home that evening, I reflected on how I was going to handle the situation the following morning. My first instinct was to tell everyone what they had done wrong. "If Johnson had bothered to turn his stories in on time, we wouldn't have been so rushed," or "If Timmons had taken better pictures, we wouldn't have had to redo so many." But I also had to admit that things would have gone more smoothly if I had had more experience, if I was more familiar with the production process. By the time I got home, I knew I was responsible for the chaos. As a leader, the Marine Corps had drilled into me, I am responsible for everything that my unit does and fails to do. This situation was my fault.

The next afternoon, I gathered my staff together. But instead of chewing them out for the late issue, I told them I was responsible for our disorganization. I could see their shoulders fall with relief. I also caught some raised eyebrows on some of the new lance corporals, who were relieved not to have the blame placed on them. "Now that you guys know it's my fault, let's talk about where we can make improvements."

Even some of the shyer Marines, who rarely offered opinions, voiced their observations and recommendations. One correspondent suggested that we move back the deadline for story layouts from Monday to Friday, giving us the weekend to work out any kinks before Wednesday's final deadline. Another suggested that correspondents be assigned filler stories on a regular basis so that we could build up a stock of articles to turn to when we encountered "holes," as we had on yesterday's issue, rather than rush around at the last minute. All good ideas that helped get us on track.

Had I turned the tables and blamed my team for the screw-ups, it's unlikely that we could have improved the process. We would have continued to operate as before, staying late the night before the deadline and rushing to pull the newspaper together. Plus, blaming my staff would have created animosity that might have made the situation worse. In the long run, it would have hurt my career more than it helped.

As a team, we immediately implemented many of the ideas that were generated. My taking responsibility up front created a climate of trust, so that everyone under my command felt comfortable offering suggestions for improvement without fear of sanctions. In addition to shifting the schedule around, I began spending more time on training. Each week we focused on a particular skill, such as grammar and punctuation, or a type of article, such as writing sports features. Over time we became a well-oiled machine that reflected positively on me as a leader.

By taking responsibility, I had little to lose and a lot to gain. Sure, telling my team that I was responsible for all of our problems was embarrassing. But I needed to produce results, and we as a team needed to move beyond the blame game. I needed my staff to help me succeed, and I wouldn't get their help if I yelled at them and put them on the defensive.

Eighteen months later, our formerly struggling newspaper received a note from the Commandant of the Marine Corps—the equivalent of our CEO. He had read our newspaper and sent it back with a handwritten note that said, "Best in Corps." We hadn't won a Pulitzer, but it sure felt like it.

> As a leader, you must take responsibility for your team's actions, whether you collectively succeed or fail. By communicating your willingness to assume that responsibility, you will create a climate in which trust and success thrive and blaming and finger-pointing are viewed as pointless.

Taking responsibility, rather than blaming others, yields results. I saw that firsthand both as a leader in the Corps and as an employee of a pharmaceutical company that I joined when I left active duty. In both situations, whether I was responsible for several people or solely for myself, taking responsibility for my actions and my work made me a leader.

SEEK SOLUTIONS INSTEAD OF PLACING BLAME

Angie

After leaving the Marine Corps, I applied my education and training in pharmaceutical sales, an industry and position that I thought would provide rewarding challenges and pay for performance. I was right that it was rewarding and challenging, yet it was also full of surprises.

My first surprise came when I joined my sales team in Los Angeles after three months of training at corporate headquarters. I was excited and ready to begin selling like crazy. I had changed from my camouflage uniform to Ann Taylor suits. There were other, more subtle differences, too. No one saluted me or called me "Ma'am," and I was now a team player, not a team leader.

When I finally met my teammates, I learned the truth about what lay ahead. Our team was consistently in the bottom quarter of the teams in our sales territory and had been for the last five years. No one on it ever made his or her annual sales quota. I had been assigned to a losing team.

Before I hit the streets, my three coworkers, Mark, Carlos, and Tamara, sat me down and gave me the inside scoop. Our territory, they told me, included some of the poorest areas of L.A., where patients didn't have the luxury of prescription coverage. Since they had to pay for medication out of their own pockets, doctors frequently wrote prescriptions for the cheaper generic form of our drugs, rather than the brand-name formula.

The key to encouraging doctors to specify our particular medication was to get face time with them, and my coworkers were increasingly unable to get it. When they stopped by a doctor's office for a brief chat, there would often be three or four other drug company representatives already sitting in the waiting room, hoping to win a few minutes of the doctor's time. Sometimes only one or two reps would land a short meeting, and the others would leave empty-handed. In those instances, the company's reputation often made the difference between getting a meeting and not getting one. Unfortunately, my teammates complained, a fellow rep on another team, Susan, who handled other drugs that our company sold, was damaging our company's standing. When she got a meeting with a doctor, she complained about the company and about her boss, damaging the company's status and reducing our ability to get face time. My coworkers were frustrated and burned out, and our team's sales rank showed it.

After hearing my more experienced teammates talk about these difficulties, I was crushed. I had really hoped to be a star at this company, but it seemed like a losing battle. Instead of being excited, I was disappointed, frustrated, and unsure of myself. But soon my Marine Corps training kicked in. "No excuses." "No blaming." "Take responsibility for your own actions." Once I put aside all my teammates' excuses for their failure, I knew that there were things I could do to improve our situation. Instead of buying into the blame, I focused on solutions.

I started by making a list of the roadblocks my teammates had pointed out. Then I began brainstorming ways to get beyond them. I tried a lot of new approaches in the first few months; some of them worked and others didn't.

For example, I looked at the typical drug rep schedule. My coworkers started calling on doctors at around 9:30 a.m., when their offices opened. I decided to try to track down the doctors before that, during their hospital rounds, which began around 7:00 a.m. By arriving at the hospital 2½ hours earlier than my colleagues usually did, I could meet with the doctors, have a cup of coffee, and get to know them a little in their own environment. I gained access. One problem solved.

I also scheduled three or four lunch appointments with physicians and staff members each week and aggressively scheduled evening programs, such as sponsored dinners and educational seminars. My colleagues and I kicked up our evening program schedule—we started having dinner with clients once a week, rather than once a month. Together, we started focusing on different ways to increase our contact with doctors.

I also learned how to use some of the tools we had at our disposal. For example, we received regular reports ranking physicians' purchases of our drugs. Although most reps totally ignored the reports, I sought out my mentor to learn how to interpret them. After his half-day tutorial, I began to read them routinely to see which offices had suddenly reduced their usage of our product, perhaps because of a competitor's offer, and which offices' sales had jumped dramatically. I knew at a glance who were our best and worst customers.

I shared everything I learned with my teammates so that we could all benefit. Over the course of the next nine months, our team communicated more regularly, shared our inventory to make sure that no one ever ran out of the samples they needed, held evening programs together, and rotated the schedule for visiting some accounts so that we could broaden our total coverage.

Our team won a new prescription sales growth competition that year—something that was practically unheard of for such an underperforming group. The change had been a switch from focusing on problems that the team members thought were out of their control to focusing on solutions that they could initiate. When I left my job, I was amazed by my team's accomplishments. Together we had shifted away from buying into excuses and become a results-oriented team. Once we started looking for solutions to our problems, we all thrived.

Don't ignore problems; instead, make it your personal responsibility to find solutions. Even generally accepted difficulties or roadblocks can be overcome. When you approach something as your problem; you'll be more focused on solving it.

STARTING THE CLIMB

Since our time in uniform, we've talked to many friends, colleagues, and workshop participants about the obstacles they encounter. We've found that everyone has his or her own 25-foot rope. For some, it's a negative boss or finding a way to move beyond a dead-end job. For others, it's making ends meet, struggling with their weight or with a toxic relationship that they are trying to end, or carving out some "me" time during a busy week. All of us have challenges, face disappointments, and feel stuck and unable to climb our 25-foot rope at times. But it doesn't have to be this way.

When you take responsibility for yourself and your actions, you're shifting your focus from blaming to problem solving. When you stop looking at everyone else's role in your success or failure and home in on what you (and only you) can do to change the situation for the better, you're working on a solution over which you have control. In order to lead change, in your personal life or in an organization, you have to take ownership of a problem and focus on situations where you can influence outcomes. Then you need to take action.

We're all human, and we all face challenges. The difference between leaders and nonleaders is how they handle those challenges. If you blame others and look beyond yourself for the reasons why something failed, you're not a leader. But if you accept responsibility, look inward for ways you can improve, and work to seek solutions instead of placing blame, you are leading from the front.

We all know what our 25-foot rope is. Blaming it won't help you overcome it, but taking responsibility will. When you take responsibility before you begin to place blame, you'll be amazed at what you can accomplish.

CHAPTER SUMMARY POINTS

- Leaders resist society's invitation to get on the "blame bandwagon." They accept responsibility for their actions and don't get bogged down in pointing fingers or placing blame elsewhere. They evaluate their own role in the situation before looking for other possible causes, as Courtney finally did to find a way up the 25-foot rope. They are also more interested in making progress than in figuring out who did what; spending more than a few minutes trying to figure out who's at fault is wasted time unless you're past the crisis and are trying to prevent future snafus. Instead, start brainstorming solutions to the problem at hand. That's much more productive.

• When you feel overwhelmed or things seem out of control, recognize that you probably had something to do with creating the chaos, and this means that you also have the power to change it. Start by delegating tasks and asking for help; who else on your team could assume some of your responsibilities? Then forge ahead to make progress on each of your current responsibilities. Finally, say no to new obligations or responsibilities until you have your current workload under control, and be honest about your existing commitments and availability.

• Leaders work to find solutions by focusing on areas where they can make a difference; they don't get distracted or waste time and energy trying to change circumstances that they can't control. Instead of focusing on how inexperienced her newspaper team was, something that she had no control over, Angie looked for ways her team could improve its performance—something that she could control. Think a change at the top of your company would do wonders? You could be right, but since you have almost no control over that scenario, spend your time considering how you could make a difference in your own department, with your own team or your customer base. Being practical can often be more productive.

• The sooner you look inward and accept responsibility for the challenges in your life, the sooner you'll overcome those challenges. Although Angie initially felt at the mercy of her poor-performing sales territory, once she started examining what

she could do to change the situation, she made incredible
progress that turned her whole team around. Likewise, once you
see that you have shaped your life as it is now, you'll also realize
that you have the power to change it. Start small, but at least
start. Own up to your problems and fix them. Look for
opportunities and pursue them. It's up to you.

CHAPTER 4

TRUE LEADERS DEDICATE THEMSELVES TO SERVICE— TAKE CARE OF THOSE YOU LEAD

Nearly everyone wants to be in charge—to be the boss, the top dog, the leader. Because when you're the leader, you get to make the rules, right? You also get power, prestige, and perks, like a bigger paycheck and an office with a door. For many, being a leader is synonymous with the benefits—tangible and intangible—of the position.

Unfortunately, leaders who place a priority on the trappings of their position, rather than on their new responsibilities and obligations, frequently aren't effective in the role. We've seen plenty of senior-level employees get so caught up in flaunting their power that they lose focus—they forget that their number one priority should be helping their organization succeed. Being too focused on "what's in it for me" also makes them less desirable as a boss or supervisor. Corporate leaders who are more concerned with the amount of publicity they're getting or the size of their annual bonus generally have problems attracting followers—people who will work hard to help them achieve success. That's because potential followers recognize how unimportant they are to this type of leader.

Leaders who spend more time worrying about meeting their own needs than about the needs of their constituents are almost guaranteed to face difficulties. When subordinates feel that they receive no respect or loyalty from those in charge, the organization's morale and culture are bound to suffer. There is frequently no camaraderie and no sense of team, and little effort is expended to assist the leader in his or her quest for glory.

Of course, leaders with that narcissistic view aren't real leaders. Contrary to popular belief, leading is not about selfishness or about getting what's due to you. Leadership is about caretaking—taking care of those around you. Being a leader certainly has privileges— the opportunity to influence outcomes and inspire others. But with those privileges comes responsibility.

Surprisingly, being a caretaker isn't that difficult. It starts with learning about those around you, getting to know them. Initiate conversations with your colleagues or employees; ask them how they are doing, how their family is, and how they spend their time outside work, for example. Remember important dates and milestones for your employees or team members, such as birthdays and anniversaries. Once you get into a routine of inquiring about others, you learn to recognize when something might be wrong, which is your opportunity to step in as leader.

If you suspect that a member of your team may need some additional support, you need to find out how you can best assist that person—you need to be part detective, part problem solver, part counselor. Is there a personal crisis that requires an employee's attention at home? Perhaps you can investigate ways to allocate personal days that will get him the time away without having to worry about his paycheck being docked. Or maybe you notice that a formerly gung-ho employee now seems rather unmotivated. As leader, it's your job to find out why and figure out how to turn her around, for her own benefit and the success of your company. Leaders look for ways to help others be successful.

Mothers are the perfect examples of caretakers. Most women who decide to have, adopt, or become a foster parent to children are instantly, instinctively, changed forever. They have suddenly become leaders, yet their first thought isn't of what they are now entitled to as a parent, it's of what they can do for their child. They recognize the importance of teaching, nurturing, and caring for their son or daughter, despite the sacrifices required by such a role. They assume the role knowing that they'll be required to be a caretaker and leader. Fortunately, the skills mothers use to care for their children are the same skills they can use to lead others. By putting the needs of others first, they create a team, a family, that is much stronger because of their leadership.

Likewise, many men and women aspire to earn the title of Marine because they want to be leaders. They want to become part of the strongest team in the world—among the proud few who uphold the Corps' motto: "Semper Fidelis—Always Faithful." Unlike the other branches of the military, which focus more on the skills of the individual, the Marine Corps' focus is on being part of a team. In the Army, you can be "An Army of One." You can "Aim High" in the Air Force, you can "Accelerate your Life" in the Navy, and you can earn money for college in the National Guard. But only in the Marine Corps is the emphasis on contributing to a success-oriented team. For that reason, the camaraderie among Marines, the loyalty to the Corps and to each other, is unmatched.

While leaders constantly look for opportunities to take care of their teams, they also need to be careful not to confuse caretaking with coddling. Coddling is about pampering and indulging; caretaking is about determining what your team needs and then helping them get it for themselves so that they can perform at their best. It's also about rewarding them before accepting honors for yourself.

TAKE CARE OF THOSE TO THE LEFT AND RIGHT OF YOU

Angie

The Corps taught me that as a leader, I was responsible for the well-being of everyone under my command—their health and safety were my priorities. On the battlefield and off, I made sure that the needs of my troops, both personal and professional, were met. That meant that lower-ranking troops moved to the head of the chow line while I brought up the rear; they ate first, and I ate what was left. I also intervened on behalf of Marines who were having problems, correcting paycheck snafus and offering advice and suggestions regarding more personal matters, such as marital difficulties.

As a new officer, I didn't fully realize the impact that my efforts had on my team. I knew my role, and I tried to fulfill it as best I could, considering each situation to see where and how I could help. I did what every officer in the Corps did—I served my troops. And I was repaid for that service with loyalty, trust, high morale, and dedication.

However, my selflessness was momentarily tested after a deployment to Australia in 1999, where I provided photojournalism support to Exercise Crocodile, a joint training exercise involving the U.S. Marine Corps and the Australian forces. I brought two combat correspondents with me from Hawaii—Corporal Robert Gomez and Corporal Paul Dodson—to help coordinate media coverage for the exercise. In the short time we were there, we developed and scheduled a "Community Day" and invited local residents to visit the base camp. The Marines had a great time showing the community members all the Marine Corps vehicles and painting the children's faces with camouflage paint. While in Australia, my team also wrote and distributed more than 100 hometown press releases for the participating troops and secured a significant amount of publicity for the unit and its work. To top it off, my commanding officer's unit was the top feature on the Marine Corps' Web site—quite a coup for him. We worked our tails off, and it showed. I left this exercise feeling proud of my professional accomplishments, as well as those of my team.

When we arrived back in Hawaii, I was told that our team had been allocated two awards and that my commanding officer wanted me to have one. It was my responsibility to choose which one of my two team members should receive the other medal and then complete the paperwork to support it.

On the one hand, I was thrilled. In the Marine Corps, earning a medal is a big deal. Other branches of the military are much more generous with their awards. The Army, for example, recognizes an average of 1 out of every 2.2 soldiers with medals each year. The Marine Corps' ratio, by comparison, is 1:16. As usual, the Marine Corps makes us work eight times harder for the same reward! And because such honors are rare in the Corps, they are that much more coveted. I hadn't earned any personal decorations for my uniform yet and really wanted something to show off my accomplishment. Many of my friends had already received medals, and I felt a little left out. This would certainly help me earn some credibility among my peers.

I definitely wanted recognition for my performance. But how could I tell one of the two corporals that his work didn't merit an award while I claimed a medal for myself? It didn't feel right. It wasn't fair, and I didn't feel comfortable doing it. If there were two awards, the two people who most deserved them were the two Marines who served under my command.

I knew I'd made the right decision, but it was confirmed when I presented each Marine with his medal. I saw the look of pride on each of their faces and knew that receiving a medal meant more to them than it would have to me. Watching them receive their medals was my reward, although I still kind of wished there were some decoration I could wear to show it—maybe a button with a count of how many medals I awarded to Marines.

After the ceremony, Corporal Dodson approached me and asked, "What award did you receive, Ma'am? If I received a Navy Achievement Medal, then you'll probably get a Navy Commendation Medal," he guessed.

A Navy Commendation Medal would have been an even higher honor than the one he had just received, but I wouldn't be receiving it. "No, Corporal, I didn't receive any honor," I told him.

"But you did so much work, Ma'am," he said, dumbfounded.

"Well, I may have come up with some ideas, but you and Corporal Gomez were the ones who made them happen, and that's what the awards are for. You're the true heroes of the deployment," I assured him.

Although I didn't receive anything to pin on my uniform that day, what I got from my team was even more valuable. Their respect, their admiration, and their dedication certainly enhanced my military career. And when I left active duty, Corporal Dodson made sure that my send-off was memorable. He coordinated the creation of a plaque in my honor, referring to me as "the guiding light of the office." It's one of my most treasured gifts from my Marine Corps experience—even more valuable than many of the medals I ultimately received during my career.

 Recognizing the work of those around you, rather than claiming credit for yourself, is the sign of a true leader. Such selfless acts produce gratitude, loyalty, and respect, which can make you an even more effective and successful leader in the long run.

REACH OUT TO YOUR TEAM MEMBERS
WHEN THEY NEED YOU

Angie

Being a caretaker was fundamental to my success as a Marine. The concept was at the core of being a leader, and I assumed that managers in the civilian world were well aware of this. Apparently, they weren't.

Caretaking is reciprocal. I knew it, and I expected other leaders to know it, too. The more I, as a leader, took care of my troops, the more they took care of me. Yet once I left the confines of the Corps, I learned that the corporate world had a different, more one-sided, view of caretaking.

By August 2003, just a few months after joining my employer, I was already one of the top 10 sales representatives in my region. I had been pouring my heart and soul into my work because my personal life was, frankly, pretty miserable. My husband, an active-duty Marine, had returned from serving in the war in Iraq in May but was then deployed to Africa for seven months beginning in July. We'd moved to North Carolina the previous year, but, because of the travel required by my work, I had few friends around to console me. Fortunately, my brother was preparing to move down to North Carolina to keep me company for the next six months while Matt was away. I was really looking forward to having Dan around.

Then I got a call from my parents that changed my life. Dan had been staying with them and was missing. So was a rifle. I was confused, but I instantly feared the worst. I flew home to Michigan immediately and alerted my husband by e-mail to what was going on. When his boss, a Marine general, learned the situation, he immediately put Matt on a plane to be with us. For five exhausting days we searched for Dan, each day hoping that he would call and put our fears to rest. On the sixth day, the sheriff's department notified us that they had located his body. Our greatest nightmare was now our reality—Dan had taken his own life.

I was beyond devastated. Nothing in my life had prepared me for this tragedy. I had experienced death before—my grandmother's, my uncle's, a few of my parents' friends—but nothing as shocking as suicide, and nothing as painful or tragic as losing a brother. The most difficult aspect of this loss was trying to make sense of my brother's death. He left no note, just a mystery that even today has not been solved. His disappearance, and, ultimately, his death, was a complete surprise to my family. We were paralyzed by our emotions, but we knew we needed to take care of each other to get through this.

The best way I could care for my family was to be a leader, to take care of myself and attempt to get back to my routine—to keep on living. I needed to be a role model for them. By taking care of myself, I could reduce the stress of those around me, allowing, and encouraging, them to focus on what they needed to do to be OK.

Matt had to return to Africa a few days later, and I headed back to North Carolina. Although I didn't feel ready to face my customers, I knew I needed to start back to work. Truthfully, the only thing that helped me get out of bed in the morning those first few days was my sense of responsibility to my husband and my family. We all needed each other to be strong, and, as a result, we forced ourselves back into our structured lives. I had hoped that the transition from mourning back to work would go smoothly, but it didn't, mainly because of my company's response to the tragedy I had just experienced.

My manager, Mike, kept his distance during my crisis; not once did he pick up the phone to express any sympathy or to see how I was doing. The only conversations we had were back-and-forth voice mail messages I initiated that went something like this:

"Hi, Mike, this is Angie Morgan. I wanted to let you know that I'm back in town. My brother's funeral was last Monday, and I expect to be back at work this week. I'm finding it difficult to think about work, and I hope you'll understand."

"Hi, Angie, it's Mike. I don't really know how to help you with your personal issues, but I'd like to talk about how I can help you with your business needs."

I was shocked by his response. My business needs? What was he talking about? Business was the absolute last thing I was thinking about. Didn't he get that? Anyway, I was one of the company's top performers—there wasn't much he could do to help me reach the top because I was already there.

"Angie, I think it would really help you to get back to work, get back to your old routine," Mike told me. "Please let me know how I can help make that happen for you."

I felt like we were having two different conversations. I was expressing the difficulty I was having thinking about selling pharmaceutical products, and he didn't want to hear it. He wanted to talk only about how quickly I was going to start selling again, driving business and meeting my sales objectives.

When I got back to work, Mike informed me that the company was going to use my remaining two weeks of vacation to cover the days I had taken off. I looked at him in disbelief. "Mike, my brother committed suicide. What I just experienced was not a vacation, it was a tragedy. If you take my remaining vacation days, I won't have any left to go home to be with my parents during the holidays. My husband is in Africa, and my family needs me. What am I supposed to do?" I blinked back tears at the thought of being home alone in North Carolina for the holidays.

Mike didn't have an answer for me, so I tried to come up with an alternative solution that preserved my vacation time. I asked, "Is there any way the company can dock my pay for the last two weeks, instead of using my vacation time?" He'd said he'd have to check and get back to me.

I learned later, through numerous phone calls to various departments, that giving personal time off for such events was at the manager's discretion. Mike could have given me more time off if he'd asked for it, but he obviously didn't think this was an important battle to fight. I also found out that the company covered the cost of counseling—something that Mike didn't even bother to inquire about. He just wanted me back at work ASAP!

The next day, my second back on the job, Mike announced that he was going to do a field evaluation with me. What a perfect time to evaluate my performance, I thought sarcastically. Although Mike did field evaluations once a month, observing me with customers and then writing up a report of my performance on the job, a week after I'd delivered my brother's eulogy didn't seem to be the appropriate time to conduct an assessment of my job performance. I hadn't expected special treatment from him, but he seemed to be going out of his way to be heartless and uncaring.

It wasn't only Mike who seemed oblivious to humane treatment of grieving employees; the lack of compassion seemed to stretch companywide. Throughout my ordeal, the company's senior managers were radio silent—no cards, no phone calls, no flowers, nothing to indicate that they knew I was hurting. I don't know what I expected from them, but I didn't anticipate that they would be so callous. Their ignoring me in my grief showed me how unimportant I was to the company. So why was I working so hard to make it successful, I began to ask myself. I was just a number to the senior managers, apparently.

I'm not proud to admit it, but my performance began to slip. Mentally, I was no longer committed to the company. It had shown how truly uncommitted it was to me. So about four months after my brother died, I began to look for a new position, and about two months after that, I was recruited by another company. I was excited to join a new company—one that not only valued my sales experience, but also had a reputation for its strong team environment.

> Failing to take care of those you lead can have damaging consequences. In addition to losing the loyalty, dedication, and motivation of your team, you may ultimately lose your team members. Strong teams have leaders who constantly look for ways to serve and assist others, especially during times of personal crisis.

I was a top performer in a company that supposedly valued and rewarded strong performers, yet my leaders didn't see any need to take care of me. As a result, they lost one of their leading employees. In contrast, when Courtney needed help, the Marine Corps went beyond her expectations.

ANTICIPATE THE NEEDS OF OTHERS

Courtney

The Marine Corps is known far and wide for its camaraderie—the "all for one and one for all" mentality that pervades the culture. The saying "once a Marine, always a Marine" reflects the sense of family and community that Marines enjoy. That sense of family is derived from a focus on others. We were trained to constantly anticipate and meet the needs of fellow Marines, and we were told to expect the same treatment if we were ever in need. When I was on active duty, I knew that I could count on the Marines around me for help, but I didn't expect the same level of care as a former Marine. It turns out that I had underestimated the Corps.

One night, when I was working late in my office at the software company where I was a sales manager, I received a phone call. My mother was on a well-deserved vacation in Spain, and I figured that she was calling to check in. She had suffered a heart attack the year before, had fully recovered, and was enjoying a respite abroad. I quickly picked up the phone to chat with her about her trip. Unfortunately, it wasn't my mother on the line.

The man on the other end of the phone identified himself in broken English as a doctor at Ramon y Cajal hospital in Madrid. My mother had apparently suffered another heart attack and was in intensive care. He said that someone from our family needed to get to Madrid as soon as possible. My heart sank as memories of my mother's past medical crises engulfed me. The pain and fear that I thought were in the past now came rushing back. "How could this be happening again," I worried.

Dazed, I quickly booked a flight and was on a plane over the Atlantic within hours of receiving the call. I took a cab from the airport to the hospital. During the entire trip to Spain, I felt as if I were racing against an unknown timer, not knowing how my mother was progressing. The idle time on the flight only caused me to think the worst. Part of me feared that she had slipped away during my flight.

I felt tremendous relief when I reached my mother's hospital room and found her groggy, but conscious. The doctors had downgraded her condition from a heart attack to a pulmonary embolism, which was being treated by blood thinners, but they said that she wouldn't be able to travel for at least five to six days. I was grateful to hear this positive prognosis, but I hadn't really thought about where I'd stay once I got to Madrid. Now that I knew I'd be there for up to a week, I had to find a hotel. I tried to get recommendations from the nurses, but they spoke little English and I no Spanish. After no success with the hospital staff, I decided to call the Marines at the U.S. Embassy, who would at least be able to understand me.

Marines provide security at most U.S. embassies worldwide, so I knew they would be able to recommend a hotel and give me pointers on making my way around the city. I placed a call through the hospital operator and was connected to the Marine on duty at the U.S. Embassy, Sergeant Wesley Parks.

"Hello, I'm a former Marine who arrived in Spain this morning to be with my mother, who became ill while traveling. She's going to be here for a few days, and I was wondering if you could recommend a hotel nearby."

His next question caught me off guard. I was expecting him to ask something to do with logistics of finding a hotel room. Instead, the sergeant expressed concern for my mother. "How is your mom doing?" he wanted to know. "Is she at Ramon y Cajal?"

When I told him she was, he assured me that it was the best hospital in the city and that she'd be well cared for. Then he told me to sit tight and he would book a room for me in the hotel directly across the street from the embassy. He would also dispatch a car to pick me up at the hospital and drive me to the hotel. After I checked in and had rested, he invited me to stop by the embassy so that he could give me all the information I needed to navigate the subway back and forth from the hospital. Here I was in a strange country, reeling from the stress of my mom's emergency, and a Marine who didn't know me at all was taking care of me. I was never so appreciative of someone's help. I had called hoping simply for administrative support in finding a decent hotel, and he had given me that plus emotional support that I didn't even know I needed. Like me, the sergeant had been trained to take care of fellow Marines. When I needed it most, he took charge of the situation and led me where I needed to go.

The next day, Sergeant Parks left me a voice mail message at the hotel: "Hello, Ma'am. I just wanted to check in to see how your mom was doing." He also told me if I needed to, I could use the phone at the embassy to make insurance arrangements and schedule our return flight. He even stopped by the hospital to meet my mom later in the week. During my week in Madrid, the Marines did everything they could to assist me. My mom's condition eventually stabilized enough so that she could fly home, and she ultimately made a full recovery.

My Marine Corps training had taught me that taking care of others was the key to building strong teams, but my experience in Madrid drove that point home. As a leader, the more you do to take care of others, to make sure their needs are met, the bigger the impact you can have on your team and your organization. I had never felt more proud to be a Marine.

There are many ways to be a caretaker, to provide support to those you lead. For instance, professionally, you can provide encouragement, guidance, and mentoring to help your team members be better employees. Personally, you can assist your employees with issues such as finances, health, family, or education. Look for ways to be of service.

You don't need to wait to offer help until someone is desperate for it. We spoke with a group of assistant principals, for example, who made a point of walking through the hallways and classrooms of their school every morning to greet teachers and students. Getting to know their staff and seeking them out every day made them more aware of important issues and let them resolve potential problems immediately—often on the spot. And all they did was ask how they could be of help each morning. They were leading from the front, not leading from their desks. Caretaking is best done in person. E-mail is great for administration, but it is a poor substitute for personal interaction.

Being a leader requires you to know your team members well enough to recognize when you can be of service. Many of these situations came up while I was sales manager at the software company.

LOOK FOR UNSPOKEN NEEDS

Courtney

As a manager, I saw my job as being a solutions provider for my employees. Whether they needed help with work or with a personal issue, I made myself available to them 24/7. Although their initial reaction to my offer of help was often surprise, they gradually understood that by taking care of each other, our team could achieve much more. So when I overhead one of my employees mention that she had been really looking forward to going out of town over the weekend, but that her dog sitter had just canceled on her, I immediately volunteered my dog expertise, limited as it was. I spent some time with her puppy over the next couple of days, and she returned from a weekend away rejuvenated and grateful.

Sometimes what my employees needed was obvious, such as a few days off to take care of an ill family member or help in negotiating a better deal on car repairs. Other times, I had to dig deeper. When one employee's performance suddenly started to decline, I sat down with him to try to find out why this solid worker was now struggling. Instead of firing him, as some managers might have done, I kept asking "why." Lo and behold, he revealed that he felt different from his coworkers, who had college degrees. Bingo! That's where I could help. I went with him to investigate local colleges, held him accountable for doing well in his courses, and completed all the paperwork to ensure that the company reimbursed his tuition. His subsequent performance surpassed his prior best results, mainly because I believed in him and gave him what he needed: support as he worked to earn a degree.

I also volunteered to help employees who aspired to be promoted. To ensure that one of my colleagues put his best foot forward, I spent hours with him creating a one-page summary of his professional accomplishments, ran through mock interviews, and shared my recommendations for how to handle questions that would inevitably be raised. When he aced his first interview, I don't know which of us was more proud.

In every situation, I tried to put myself in my employees' shoes to see what I, as their leader, could do that would help the most. In exchange for the time I invested in each of my employees, I received their gratitude, their dedication, and their trust. The result was a cohesive team that surpassed my expectations.

> A strong leader does not limit him- or herself to caring for teammates solely on professional issues, especially when those issues may have been brought on by personal challenges. Leaders look for the root cause of problems and then seek solutions in order to help their team and the individuals who are part of it.

When you sincerely focus on the needs of those you lead, you inspire the confidence and level of commitment they need if they are to be successful.

LEADERS NEED BALANCE, TOO

Women are frequently natural leaders and caregivers. They're very adept at recognizing when someone needs help and offering it. However, sometimes they're not as adept at recognizing their own limitations. Many women have a tendency to go overboard when it comes to helping, and some lose sight of themselves. They have so many roles to fill that they put themselves last, but over time that leads to weakness. Leaders can't lead when they haven't been taking care of themselves, too.

There's a difference between selflessness and self-neglect. Being selfless means that you help others get what they need if they are to be successful, but you can't totally ignore your own needs. Lending your car to a friend so that she can buy groceries is selfless, but only if you don't rely on your car to get to work. Similarly, buying your teenager nice school clothes is great, as long as you don't have to max out your credit cards to pay for them. Your needs count, too. It's a delicate balance.

And that's the tricky part about being a leader. To be most effective, you need to balance the needs of others with your own needs. By prioritizing the many demands that others place on your time and including your own need for time to relax and rejuvenate, you'll be ready to lead when you see a need, or an opportunity.

It's quite an accomplishment to become a leader. But the best leaders understand that with their role comes the responsibility for helping their team perform at its best. A leader fails when they revel in their newfound power and prestige and forget about the people who helped them get there.

You can be a strong leader by taking care of yourself and those around you. It's important to balance your efforts in both areas so that neither is neglected. Ultimately, teams and organizations are most successful when their leader works for the team. In exchange for their support and assistance, leaders earn the respect and best effort from those around them. It's a win-win situation.

CHAPTER SUMMARY POINTS

- Leaders are caretakers, not bosses. They place a higher priority on serving their team than on grabbing all the potential benefits of their position, such as more money, more perks, and more power. Leaders constantly recognize and demonstrate how important those under their command are to them and their mission, as Angie did by giving the two medals she'd been allocated to her Marines, rather than taking one for herself.

- Leaders don't coddle, however. They don't pamper and indulge, but they do work hard to learn what their team needs and then do their best to get it, whether what's needed is equipment, time, or guidance. Courtney's efforts to help an employee earn the college degree he so desperately wanted stopped short of coddling—she helped him scope out college programs and get the paperwork done to get reimbursement from the company, but she didn't drive him to class or help him with his homework. Part of the responsibility for achieving success still has to rest with the individual, not the leader.

- Don't wait for team members to ask for help—be on the lookout for opportunities to offer your assistance. Angie's manager had a prime opportunity to assist when he learned of her brother's suicide. Unfortunately, he missed the chance to be a leader. The better you know your employees, family members, and friends, the easier it will be to anticipate their needs.

- Putting your team's needs before your own earns their respect and loyalty. Such dedication can significantly enhance your life. But there is a fine line between supporting your team and neglecting your own needs. Your team may need you to put in some extra hours on a big project, but if you're already working 60-hour weeks, piling on more hours may not be the best way for you to contribute. Look for a balance. Taking care of yourself is also part of being a strong leader.

CHAPTER 5

THINK BEFORE YOU ACT— ESPECIALLY BEFORE YOU OVERREACT

Leaders are more than caretakers—they also model good behavior. Those who approach situations rationally and respond to new information unemotionally are more effective, because of the confidence that develops within their team. Those around them trust them to remain calm, cool, and collected, even when faced with a crisis.

It's much easier to have faith in a leader who remains calm in the face of chaos. The leader's reaction sets the standard for everyone else's reaction, which is good news when a true leader is in charge and bad news when someone who is more easily flustered is at the helm. Unfortunately, women often have more difficulty keeping their emotions in check and are more likely to get flustered.

Some women we've worked with say that it is hard for them to control their impulses—they get caught up in their emotions and find it hard to suppress those emotions. Unfortunately, women whose emotions are out of control often have a bad reputation at the office, one that will certainly damage their efforts to influence outcomes and inspire others.

Rightly or wrongly, women are stereotyped as being overly emotional, or at least more emotional than men. Granted, this reputation isn't always deserved, but in many cases emotional behavior is expected. Women are perceived as being more likely to display their emotions in public than men, and that perception can interfere with their ability to lead. When a woman becomes emotional, she's seen as weak or a "drama queen," whereas men displaying similar emotions are "passionate." Such gender differences certainly aren't fair, but women need to be aware of them in order to counter them.

People want leaders who are strong, who display confidence, and who can keep their emotions in check—in any situation. Not only is a breakdown embarrassing to witness, but it's also unproductive and unprofessional. No one wants to see a leader throw a tantrum, or to be faced with yelling or angry outbursts. Emotional leaders shape the professional environment they work in. When Angie worked in pharmaceuticals, she could always tell what type of doctor worked in the office even before she met him or her solely by how the receptionist received her. If the receptionist was blunt and somewhat abusive to the sales reps, Angie knew the doctor was a screamer. If the receptionist was gracious, the doctor was typically friendly. Overreacting to staff members only damages the leader's reputation and makes others less interested in working for him or her.

Outside of work, the same leadership principles apply. If you overreact, you'll lose the respect and confidence of those around you, and thus damage your ability to influence outcomes—to be a leader. Say, for instance, your son confides in you that he tried smoking with some friends after school. If you become angry and yell at him, he's not likely to share such information with you in the future. You've effectively cut off communication with your troops. A leader needs to know how to handle bad or unexpected news.

Staying calm allows you to think more clearly and not get side-tracked by emotion. The more emotional and upset you are, the less able you are to think through your options and formulate a plan for success. That's true whether you're facing an attack on a battlefield or dealing with an injured child who needs to get to the hospital.

Your ability to remain composed will also encourage those around you—everyone from your employees to your spouse—to give you all the information you need to address a situation. When people trust you not to fly off the handle, they are much more comfortable giving you a complete picture of what has happened or is happening. They don't need to water it down to avoid an emotional outbreak. Your reputation for being even-tempered will encourage complete disclosure. It will also attract followers.

In the Marine Corps, we were told to "save the drama for your mama" whenever our sergeant instructors sensed that we were getting too worked up about our field training. They would scream at us, put their face within inches of ours as they yelled, pummel us with a steady stream of instructions and commands, and punish our bodies with constant exercise. But the point of the training wasn't to wear us out. The point was to teach us how to perform under duress. During high-intensity situations, we became acclimated to keeping our "bearing" at all times, our bearing being our ability to "create a favorable impression in carriage, appearance, and personal conduct." That meant being able to put our emotions aside to deal with the challenge at hand—anything from being attacked by the enemy to juggling 10 high-priority work assignments at once.

No matter what, we had to focus on solutions, not on our instinctive reaction of fear, anxiety, or anger. Our troops looked to us for inspiration and guidance. Extreme emotional responses interfered with our ability to build confidence and to lead. Courtney saw that first-hand during The Basic School, when she worked alongside a woman who was incapable of keeping her emotions in check.

EMOTIONAL OUTBURSTS
DESTROY YOUR CREDIBILITY

Courtney

Lisa Randall, the only other woman in my unit, was an extremely talented Marine. She was an expert shot, could navigate her way through the trickiest combat scenarios, and had the cleanest rifle you could imagine—a true accolade in the Corps. Her military skills were far superior to those of most of the Marines on our team. Her only apparent weakness was her inability to control her emotions under stress. Unfortunately, that weakness overshadowed her many strengths.

Her habit of freaking out had earned her the nickname "Fly Off the Handle Randall" from the rest of our platoon, who had come to expect tirades and breakdowns from her. Her inability to control her emotions lost her the respect of the other members of the platoon, who eventually stopped listening or paying attention to her. No one wanted to deal with her emotional outbursts, which made it nearly impossible for her to lead.

As her roommate on base, I knew how knowledgeable she was and how serious she was about being a Marine, but after one night attack, even I began to wonder if she would ever be able to squelch her outbursts and become a leader.

Lisa was leading the mission that night, which was to assault an objective in the woods and then make an exit via helicopter a short distance away. We made the assault fine, but then got lost on our way to the helicopter's landing zone. Technically, this was the fault of the Marine doing the land navigating, but ultimately, it was Lisa's job as leader to get us back on course. It's hard to keep track of everyone in the dark, and it's even more difficult to stay on course without any visible landmarks. I was moving through the brush on Lisa's left and could hear her conversation with Lieutenant Martin, the guy doing the land navigating. I could tell she was feeling the pressure because her voice was getting louder and angrier. At night in the woods, sound carries easily, so you need to speak in barely above a whisper to avoid being heard. If our instructor heard her arguing, she would immediately fail the exercise.

I knew she needed help, so I flung my rifle over my shoulder and left my position to join the discussion. Lieutenant Martin was an excellent navigator, so it was a fluke that he had gotten lost. Lisa knew this, yet she was berating him. In response, he rolled his eyes and told her, "Shut up and pull yourself together." Since we all wore the same rank, he couldn't be penalized for his insubordination, but his comment added fuel to her emotional fire. She continued her tirade, raising her voice well above the hushed tones required in the situation. Finally, Lieutenant Martin had had enough and stormed off, telling her, "Find your own way out of your mess." Great; now she'd lost the support of the Marine in our unit most qualified to find the helicopter's landing zone.

Lisa and I were left holding the map. We both knew that land nav is not my forte—Lieutenant Martin had the compass for a reason—but instead of trying to figure out where we were and calm down, she began complaining to me. "Let's just focus on a solution," I suggested. "We can talk about what happened later. Right now you need to be quiet." Finally, she shut up.

A few minutes later, still not knowing where we were, I heard the whoosh, whoosh of helicopter blades. Although we hadn't yet found the helicopter's landing zone, it was nearby. We could make our way there by following the sound. I made a command decision:

"Lisa, get the unit moving," I told her. "I have no idea where we are on the map, but let's head in the direction of the helicopter."

She worked quickly, calming herself as she issued orders to the troops. Together we got them moving and on board the helicopter, but we were 20 minutes behind schedule. We'd made it to our destination, but the delay was a big error. As Marines training for war, we were taught repeatedly that any delay can be deadly. Had the helicopter's landing zone been "hot," meaning that enemy forces had surrounded it, that lost time could have cost lives. I thought about this on the short trip home and how Randall's emotional outburst had interfered with the mission.

By the time we reached the base, Lieutenant Martin had already told most of the platoon how "Fly Off the Handle Randall" had underperformed again. Although she was technically and tactically more proficient than many in our unit, she was consistently ranked dead last by our colleagues during periodic peer reviews. Many didn't feel she had the skills necessary to lead because they couldn't see past her inability to keep her emotions in check.

I was in the unusual position of both observing Lisa's military know-how as her roommate and hearing assessments of her performance—or lack thereof—from our platoon-mates. From that vantage point, I was well aware of the negative impact her losing her cool had on her reputation and ability to lead—perhaps more aware than she was. I saw how her temper tantrums alienated those under her command and how she brought out the worst in people through her ranting and raving. Instead of leading, she drove people away. For that reason, few Marines ever realized the talents that Lisa actually had.

I learned a lot about being a leader from Lisa. I saw how her overreacting was contagious, leading her teammates to overreact in response to her behavior. I saw how her troops discounted her abilities because of her reactions and interactions. I saw how her emotions paralyzed her, and I worked that much harder to keep my own emotions under control.

When you overreact, you alienate your team and lose their trust and respect. Extreme emotions are a roadblock to success; learning to control them is essential to your success as a leader.

Angie is quite good at keeping her emotions in check, but on a couple of occasions in the Corps, she had to work hard to remain calm. Luckily, she learned that when you distance yourself from an emotional situation, you're able to gain a clear perspective. You're also able to handle the situation with a more controlled demeanor.

PROFESSIONALISM REQUIRES THAT YOU STEP AWAY FROM THE SITUATION

Angie

During my last year in Hawaii, I was handpicked for a new assignment as the base's protocol officer. Although it was an honor, I was not happy about it. I would much rather have been out in the field leading troops. Instead, I was stuck at a desk job as a glorified party planner, ordering sheet cakes, sending out invitations, making up seating charts for base parades, and preparing handwritten pillow notes for visiting VIPs (yes, I actually wrote little messages and laid them on the pillows of our guests to make them feel welcome). It was almost embarrassing to hear about the daring adventures my friends were having overseas, but I tried to see my current job as an opportunity. Until one day I felt I'd hit rock bottom career-wise.

In early December, General Mitchell's aide de camp (his assistant), Kristy Lewis, came to my office to tell me I was needed at the general's home that Friday night to help his wife, Tina, with her Christmas party. Apparently, Tina was participating in the Officers' Wives Club tour of homes on the base, where the officers' wives spend weeks decorating their homes for the holidays so that the other wives can come and admire their handiwork. My assignment, she told me, was to help the members with their coats and then provide a tour of all the decorations in Tina's home, allowing guests sufficient time to admire her nativity scene, drool over her Christmas china, and marvel over her neatly trimmed tree.

I thought she was joking.

"While I can certainly appreciate a good holiday tour of homes, I don't appreciate the order to serve as host at the main tour attraction. While I'm there, would Tina also like me to provide on-site pedicures for her guests, painting tiny holly boughs on their toenails to get them into the holiday spirit?" I asked sarcastically.

"I'm serious, Angie. The general wants you at that party," she told me, frowning a little.

"I'm serious, too. This is ridiculous!" I responded. "I'm the general's protocol officer, not his wife's personal assistant or maid. This sounds a little like personal servitude, which is a borderline unlawful order. As a Marine Corps officer, I shouldn't be asked to participate in such an event. Did Tina put you up to this?" I asked pointedly.

"No, General Mitchell asked that you and I both be present at the party," she said. "This request is coming from him, not his wife."

Normally, I'm good at keeping my cool, but I could feel my temper rising as I considered this unusual request. I couldn't believe I was being asked to give up my Friday night for such a menial job. This was way beyond my job description, and I was seriously offended. If I had been a guy, there's no way the general would have asked me to do this, I assumed. And yet, he *had* asked. So what could I do now?

"Kristy, can I talk to the general to understand what my official role is at the party? As a Marine, if the general had asked me to be at his house on a Friday night to set up a trip wire, position snipers on the roof, and prepare a defensive position, I wouldn't question my role for a minute. But I don't understand how helping out at his wife's holiday party is part of my official Marine Corps responsibilities. I serve the Marine Corps and General Mitchell, but when I last checked, I don't serve his wife," I continued.

"The general is out of the office for the rest of the afternoon, but you can meet with him first thing tomorrow morning," she told me, adding, "I suggest you take until then to pull yourself together. You may also want to use some tact when addressing the general, which right now, I think you'd have difficulty mustering."

She was right, of course. I was so wound up, so angry that General Mitchell had made a request that seemed way out of line that I needed a few hours to sort out what exactly I was going to say to him. What was I going to ask him? Whatever it was, I needed to be sure that it didn't come across as disrespectful—showing disrespect to any senior officer, especially a general, is the quickest way to a reduction in rank and pay. I decided I needed to focus on getting a clarification of my official Marine Corps responsibilities at the party, avoiding any suggestion that I was accusing him of making me his wife's personal servant, although that was exactly how I felt.

I knew that I had to calm down before I met with General Mitchell in the morning. That evening, I worked on separating my emotions from my legitimate concerns. I had never questioned someone's order before and knew I was on dangerous ground. What exactly did I need him to explain to me? Why was his request unusual? And how could I question his order without sounding insubordinate? I felt that his request was outrageous, but I couldn't come right out and say that. During the next few hours, in preparation for my meeting with the general, I made notes of my duties as protocol officer and compared them with what he was asking me to do. I focused on my duties, not my reaction to his order.

The next morning I reported to the general's office. He asked what was going on.

"Sir, I'm confused about why I'm needed on Friday night at your wife's party. I wasn't aware that a protocol officer's job duties included this type of work, and I thought I should get some clarification of my orders," I told him calmly.

General Mitchell looked surprised, which at first concerned me, but then I saw him flash an understanding smile.

"You know, Angie, I once served as a protocol officer for a senior Marine Corps officer, and I really didn't like it at all," he told me. "I had to go to these parties, take people's coats, and pretend that I enjoyed giving up my evenings to be there. And I, too, questioned my official responsibilities at those events. It felt like it was outside my scope of responsibility. But my superior back then explained to me that anything that happens at the general's house is an 'official' command event, and therefore I was expected to attend.

"Now, normally, I wouldn't have asked you to attend the Christmas party, but I was the one who roped my wife into participating because I thought it was a good event to be part of. As it turns out, I'll be out of town later this week and won't be able to be there. Which is why I would appreciate it if you and Kristy would both go and assist her." Then he smiled and said, "If you don't say yes, I'll have to order you to be there."

Of course, I said yes. I also thanked him for clarifying why I was needed there. Having been given several hours overnight to calm down and consider the general's request, I was able to have a professional, unemotional conversation with him about what I was being asked to do. Had I gone in upset and angry, as I had been initially, the result would have been damaging to my career. Instead, I humbly fulfilled my obligations at the holiday tour of homes, hanging coats and passing out hors d'oeuvres like a champ.

When you feel your emotions rising, take a step back or get away for at least a few minutes to regain your composure. Taking some time to clear your head and analyze the situation will help you be more effective when making your points. Once you've calmed yourself, have a levelheaded discussion. Don't allow feelings of anger, frustration, or sadness to dictate how you respond to situations that arise. An even temper is a sign of a true leader.

Keeping your cool rather than overreacting helps maintain important professional and personal relationships. Not long ago, Courtney recognized that her overreacting to some situations was beginning to have an effect on one of her most trusted teammates—her husband. While keeping your cool at the office is key to maintaining your professional relationships, it's even more important at home, where personal relationships are involved.

OVERREACTING PUTS OTHERS ON THE DEFENSIVE

Courtney

I had always thought that I was pretty good at controlling my emotions, but after a recent business trip, it became obvious that although I was ultra-professional at work, I had a tendency to overreact at home.

After giving a leadership training session at Wal-Mart, I managed to catch an earlier flight home and arrived two hours sooner than I (or my husband, apparently) had anticipated. When I pulled into the driveway, I noticed that the garbage cans were still sitting at the curb from the trash pick-up two days before, so I pulled them in. I was mildly annoyed that the cans hadn't been moved to the backyard sooner, but I was more tired than anything else and headed inside. When I walked into the house, it seemed a little messier than normal, so I started to straighten things up while I waited for Patrick to get home. I was tired, but I made good progress on the cleaning that needed to be done.

Thirty minutes later, Patrick walked through the door with a sheepish grin on his face. His plan to take care of his share of the chores before I got home had been spoiled by my early arrival. He was busted, and he knew it.

"Hi, honey, you're home awfully early," he said with a guilty smile. "I was just coming home to straighten up the house a bit and pull the garbage cans in." He was clearly nervous about the condition the house was in, and all I could do was laugh. He had expected me to be upset about his cleaning, or lack thereof, I realized, because that was how I always reacted. He went on the defensive immediately to try to prevent me from overreacting. "He must think of me as such a chore monger," I thought to myself. Here I was home early, and instead of being happy to see me, he was worried about my reaction to the chores that hadn't been done.

His greeting taught me a lesson and forced me to consider other instances where I put my husband on the defensive. My becoming upset about his failure to complete chores was creating an unhealthy dynamic in our marriage. Fortunately, once I acknowledged my tendency to get upset, we were able to talk calmly and rationally about the chores, and how we could communicate better about other aspects of our life. I needed to rein in my emotions about things like neglected chores so that Patrick wouldn't feel defensive about such a minor issue.

About a week later, when I arrived home from another business trip, I was stunned to find the house immaculate. Wow! Patrick had tackled everything, from laundry to vacuuming to dusting. I couldn't have done a better job. Not sure what had caused his newfound clean streak, I jokingly asked him what had motivated him to do all the cleaning. He told me that just as I had recognized my tendency to overreact to undone chores, he had recognized his own tendency to be messy and had decided he needed to change.

Patrick's expectation that I would flip out over the messy house reminded me of the importance of keeping my cool at work *and* at home. I hadn't initially noticed that I was overreacting about housekeeping duties, but when I did, I was able to see the impact it had: he became defensive—not a good reaction to get from your spouse. Fortunately, by applying the same leadership lesson at home (keeping my emotions in check), we were able to have a great discussion, both about the dishes that needed washing and about our relationship.

> Recognize that overreacting to situations puts others on the defensive. To deal with problems effectively, approach others calmly, with an open mind toward a solution. Keeping your emotions in check will encourage honest suggestions and helpful solutions, whereas overreacting will only discourage anyone from speaking up or participating.

Some situations need to be addressed head-on, such as misunderstandings with people you're close to. Facing issues helps you resolve and move past them, just as Patrick and I were able to do. However, other situations are better ignored or laughed off, such as the time Angie was broadsided by a put-down.

SOME SITUATIONS DON'T DESERVE A REACTION

Angie

Like Courtney, I try hard to keep my cool in all situations, but some are more difficult than others. Take a recent party I attended, for example, where I had to keep my emotions under control following an eyebrow-raising remark.

My husband, Matt, and I had been invited to a lovely reception hosted by Matt's boss, a Marine Corps general. Most of the attendees were Marine Corps officers and their spouses, and it seemed that everyone there had some connection with the Corps, which makes this story even more amusing. At some point during the evening, I began chatting with a young lieutenant and his new wife about their recent wedding. They were eager to talk about their relationship and how they had ended up at the altar, so I asked how they had met.

The young lieutenant told a very sweet story about how he had to muster the courage to invite his future wife to a formal at his college fraternity. I smiled after hearing the tale and asked how they had decided to get married.

The lieutenant explained that when he graduated from college, he faced a life-altering choice. He was going into the Marine Corps, and he believed that this decision might result in their breaking up. He asked her to marry him because he believed he would never meet a woman of her caliber in the Corps. "After all," he asked me, "have you ever seen a woman Marine before?"

"In fact, I have," I told him with a straight face, not quite sure where he was going with his question.

"Well, then you understand," he said. "They're just nasty girls—horrible! Absolutely nothing to look at."

I had a millisecond to sort out my response to his insult. Then I calmly replied, "I was a Marine."

I would pay money to see the look of absolute horror on his face again as he tried to remove his foot from his mouth. His wife, along with the small crowd around us, roared with laughter at his gaffe as he desperately tried to explain that I was attractive, I didn't fit the stereotype, and that he by no means meant to suggest that I was in any way ugly.

Although still reeling from his slight, I managed to say, "Wow. I guess you never know who you're talking to," and casually walked away.

Sure, I was shocked by his pronouncement, and a million insults that I could have hurled back at him came to mind. I could have become visibly offended and emotional at his biting remark, but what would that have accomplished? Nothing. Instead, I didn't take it personally or seriously, although I must admit I enjoyed pointing out his major blunder, and went on to enjoy the rest of the evening. Had I lashed out or overreacted, I could have made the situation much worse—the evening could have been ruined for my husband, the young couple, the other guests, and me. It wouldn't have been worth it. I had no control over the lieutenant's put-down, but I could control my own response to his tactless remark. That's what leaders do.

> In situations where you don't have the option of walking away and contemplating a levelheaded response, envision the consequences of lashing out in reaction to an insult or put-down. In most cases, you can damage relationships and your reputation as a leader with a single retort. Opt for restraint or silence to maintain your professional image.

BEHAVING LIKE A LEADER

Effective leaders are role models in many ways, including how they conduct themselves during stressful times. Being able to calmly gather information and begin working on a solution rather than having to stop and have an emotional breakdown will surely affect what happens next. An ability to control your emotions, even when they are raging internally, keeps those around you calmer, maintains professional relationships, and positions you as the go-to person when there is an emergency of some sort—people turn to those who are more likely to be even-tempered rather than to those are apt to go off half-cocked. It's human nature to avoid pain!

If you find your emotions rising, it's always best to take a step back or excuse yourself from the situation to regain your composure. That's a smart strategy, whether you're in the middle of a staff meeting, in a conversation with a state trooper who's pulled you over, or responding to the red lipstick you've just discovered your daughter used as a crayon to draw on your car's leather seats. The classic "pause and count to 10" is good advice no matter where you are or whom you're dealing with. After taking a break or getting away, you'll find that you can see the situation in a different light, without interference from your emotions.

Overreacting damages your professional reputation, loses you the respect of your employees and colleagues, interferes with personal relationships, and may even contribute to higher blood pressure. It's not a healthy way to communicate, and it's not leadership behavior.

Leaders learn to focus on the information that's been conveyed and keep their own personal reactions in check. They can then determine the best course of action and move their team ahead.

CHAPTER SUMMARY POINTS

- A composed leader sets the tone for the team's behavior. Keeping emotions in check under stress helps a leader maintain a calm team. Conversely, an out-of-control, emotional leader is likely to have a team of overreactors.

- You can't change how other people act, or overreact, but you can change your response to their outbursts. Remaining calm can help people regain their composure, so that you can have a meaningful—and less heated—discussion.

- Extreme emotions cloud your judgment, making it difficult to think clearly. Remaining calm allows you to do a better job of thinking through your various options and formulating a plan. Lisa Randall's inability to control her emotions during training prevented her from achieving success. Had she been able to remain calm, rather than berating her teammates, she would have performed much better all around. She might also have been perceived as the leader she was trying to be and the technical expert she was.

- Emotional reactions to information discourage full disclosure and can interfere with your ability to lead. When team members are made to feel uncomfortable or threatened by a leader's behavior, they may hold back on details to avoid a major outburst. Courtney discovered that she had been overreacting to undone work around the house, and that this was interfering with her relationship with her husband. Once she recognized her behavior and resolved to change it, their relationship improved.

- Overreacting to situations damages your credibility and reduces the confidence others have in you. Emotionality will overshadow your talents and abilities.

- When you feel yourself becoming too emotional, take a step away from the situation and gain a new perspective. Your clear mind will help you respond to the situation with an appropriate amount of emotion, all the while avoiding a professionally embarrassing scenario. Between the time Angie was told that her boss wanted her to assist at a Christmas party and the next morning, when she met with him to discuss his request, she had a chance to calm down and plan how she would inquire about his order without sounding upset. By remaining calm, she was able to have a frank but productive conversation with the general without receiving a reprimand for insubordination.

CHAPTER 6

WHEN FACED WITH A CRISIS— AVIATE, NAVIGATE, COMMUNICATE

Crises come in all shapes and sizes. They can occur in all sorts of situations, often at the worst possible moment—and typically when you're least expecting them. Crises often bring productive work to a halt. They create mayhem. They breed anxiety. And they test the skills of the most accomplished leader. Because a crisis is a situation that you don't immediately know how to handle, the solution—the remedy—isn't obvious.

Lower-than-expected sales, a lawsuit out of the blue, a sudden round of layoffs—crises at work generally result in a major change in workload. The feeling of being overwhelmed can send workers at all levels into a panicked tailspin. Many find it difficult to function, so they freeze. They're paralyzed by the information they've received and don't know what to do about it, so they do nothing. They hide away or deny that there is a problem, hoping that they'll eventually come up with a solution or, better yet, that the situation will resolve itself without their involvement. However, involvement is exactly what is required.

Crises are not limited to the workplace; they can erupt just as easily at home or at school. Avoiding a crisis by ignoring it isn't practical and may even make things worse. Though burying one's head in the sand can be appealing at times, it is not what a leader does. Leaders take action to improve a critical situation, whatever it is. They know that it's not wise, or practical, to stop everything and focus solely on the crisis, so they continue with what they're doing while they devise a plan to resolve the issue. They rely on a practiced system for solving the problem. In the Marine Corps, we referred to this system as "aviating, navigating, and communicating."

Aviating, navigating, and communicating describe what a pilot does when facing an airborne emergency. The first thing he or she has to do is to keep the plane flying—aviate. Then the pilot has to continue on the planned course while searching for a solution—he or she has to navigate. Once the pilot finds a solution, he or she has to communicate it to everyone involved, including air traffic control, the ground crew, and the commanding officer.

Many people we've spoken to admit that the "communicate" step of this principle is the most difficult for them. For some, the most challenging part is asking for help. Others hate admitting to their boss that they are overloaded or can't handle the work they've been given. However, the solution to a crisis requires having that difficult conversation.

Communicating is important for a number of reasons. First, it alerts those around you to the existence of a crisis. Without your telling them, they might not know about it. Second, those who knew about the crisis are now aware that you're handling it and should view you as a point of contact if they have additional information or assistance to offer. When people try to handle a crisis by themselves, they may overlook a potential solution; by involving others, you can tap into a wealth of experience and perspectives that can prove extremely valuable. Dealing with a crisis in a vacuum isn't wise, and leaders certainly don't cut themselves off from others when trying to address a problem.

Essentially, a leader keeps going, makes any needed adjustments to the flight, and lets everyone know what's going on in order to work toward a solution. That's good advice in any situation.

One group of administrative assistants we recently met with revealed that their boss and some of their boss's colleagues thought nothing of dumping extra work on their desks. These women were known as the "go-to girls" by those in their division because they routinely handled massive amounts of work. But these women were also feeling overwhelmed and had reached a point where they could no longer complete all the incoming tasks. We advised them to have a frank conversation with their boss, telling him exactly what their current workload consisted of and asking for help in prioritizing what was of critical importance. They could do anything, just not everything at once, and they needed to communicate that to their boss. Being honest about their limitations would help prevent such pileups from occurring in the future and help their boss better delegate the workload.

Sometimes you may not be aware that you're in a crisis. You may not immediately realize that you're dealing with a situation that has potentially serious consequences. However, there are indicators to watch for. If you find yourself constantly feeling pressed for time, unable to juggle all your daily commitments, or overwhelmed by everything going on around you, you may already be in crisis mode. Fortunately, once you realize you're in a crisis, you can begin aviating, navigating, and communicating like a leader to get your head above water and deal with the crisis. During a tour in the Australian Outback, Angie had a bit to learn about crisis management. Fortunately, she had Major Eric Ryder to help her maintain her focus as she searched for three Marines whom she had realized were missing.

KEEP TAKING ACTION
UNTIL THE SITUATION IS RESOLVED

Angie

"Ma'am, there's going to be a night attack near North Zone 1, and we are trying a new tactic. I'd like the combat correspondents to cover the story," Sergeant Major Lopez told me. "Mind if I borrow Gomez and Dodson for some coverage?"

"Certainly you can have them, Sergeant Major, but they haven't returned yet from covering the earlier infantry exercises," I told him.

"Weren't they supposed to be back by now?" he asked, a little surprised.

"Yes, they were. And right now I don't know exactly where they are, but they should be back soon," I said. His remarks prompted me to quickly analyze the situation.

Gomez and Dodson were actually more than four hours overdue back at our base camp in the Australian Outback, and we'd had no contact with them since early that morning. Once I realized this, I began to worry, picturing their Humvee overturned on the side of a road or lost on one of the millions of dirt roads here. It had been scorching hot, and I found myself hoping that they at least had enough water with them.

We were in the Outback training for war. My team of combat correspondents and I were there to provide coverage of the multinational training exercise for the Marine Corps at large, as well as base newspapers and *Leatherneck Magazine*. I also had to oversee Australian media access to the Marine units involved in the exercise, coordinating requests to become embedded—essentially, to enter the fray—with the units. My primary responsibility, however, was training my team for work as correspondents under actual combat conditions. They were becoming accustomed to lugging cameras along with their packs and rifles, but could use more time in the field learning about the roles and responsibilities of infantry Marines. So midexercise, I decided to embed two correspondents with an infantry unit. Corporal Robert Gomez and Corporal Paul Dodson were excited about getting some more time with the "grunts," and I asked the colonel's driver, who had been made available to me that day, to take the two men out to the main unit's fighting position to get some combat camera experience. He assured me that he knew exactly where to take Gomez and Dodson, so shortly after reveille at 5:00 a.m., they headed out. Then I went on with my other responsibilities.

While I had expected them to return earlier in the afternoon, I had assumed that they were having too much fun with the unit they were with and didn't want to return yet. It was right around this time that the sergeant major approached me about borrowing the correspondents to photograph the attack that night. When I told him that they weren't back yet, he asked if we could radio them back early—the colonel, his boss, wanted to get them in place so that they wouldn't miss the opportunity to cover the night attack. Radioing them in early was fine with me, I explained, but I wasn't sure they had a radio with them. The sergeant major looked at me, stunned.

"Lieutenant, do you understand how vast the training area is and how easy it is to get lost?" he asked.

"Yes, I know it's huge," I told him. "But the driver has been navigating these roads for weeks, so I'm not too concerned. He knows his way around, even if Gomez and Dodson don't." But inside, I had an increasingly bad feeling about the situation. Why weren't they back?

I headed to the operations center tent to see what I could do to radio them in. Once there, I pulled aside my mentor, Major Ryder, gave him a quick synopsis of the situation, and asked for advice on how to proceed. When I get nervous, I tend to talk more quickly. When I started briefing Major Ryder, I was talking so fast that he had no idea what I was saying, but he knew I was worked up over something. "Calm down, Angie. Take a deep breath. OK, now tell me what's up," he said. He first focused on getting me to calm down so that I could think and communicate more clearly.

After I communicated the situation, he began helping me generate solutions. He suggested that we call the infantry unit the correspondents were supposed to be covering to get a report on their location. We called the infantry unit without difficulty, but they reported that they hadn't seen any combat cameramen all day. I could feel my heart rate picking up again. My Marines had been gone all day—if the infantry unit hadn't seen them, then where could they be?

Major Ryder could sense by the worried look on my face that I was about to panic, so he told me, "Angie, it's possible that they got sidetracked. If you look at the map, you'll notice that there are a lot of Marine units in the bush right now. Maybe your Marines linked up with another unit along the way. Why don't we start calling those other units? Go tell the sergeant major to tell the colonel that you've got the situation under control and are reaching out to a couple other units to locate your Marines. While you do that, I'll start making some calls."

After I relayed the message to the sergeant major, I returned to check on Major Ryder's progress. He'd had no success in locating the Marines. My impulse was to get on the radio immediately and alert all units in the area to halt their activity because we had three missing Marines. Before I could act, Major Ryder reminded me that we were involved in an international exercise, and all we knew was that three Marines were late. There wasn't yet cause to sound the alarm and bring the exercise to a halt, he reasoned. Stopping an exercise that involved thousands of troops in a hasty manner would be difficult and dangerous.

The major offered a perspective I needed to hear. He was concerned, but not ready to call out the search-and-rescue helicopters and shut down the exercise immediately as I was; he wanted to start with some basic local searches, which we could expand if the Marines weren't found nearby. He helped me focus on continuing to manage our existing responsibilities—aviating—while also developing a plan to find the Marines.

His "pep talk" helped ground me. No longer in panic mode, I started to focus more on a solution. My navigation efforts kicked in as Major Ryder and I began brainstorming a systematic way to track down the missing Marines. He reminded me that we needed measures that were appropriate to the scenario. We had to start at the ground level and work our way up, asking for help from area troops before we called out search-and-rescue helicopters. Shooting a mouse with an elephant gun wasn't called for, especially since we didn't even know that they were in trouble. Incremental escalation of a search effort was more appropriate and safer.

I started by calling together some drivers and asking for their help. Several vehicles headed out to canvass the perimeter of the base camp, on the lookout for a possible accident involving the missing Humvee. I also radioed other units in the field to keep their eyes open for three combat cameramen.

Throughout the search, I kept the sergeant major informed, and he relayed those messages to the colonel. At no point did the exercise pause—there was too much underway and no reports that the Marines were in imminent danger. I had media embedded with other Marine units that I needed to coordinate, as well as my public affairs duties; I simply added efforts to track down the three Marines to my list of responsibilities. Alternating between responsibilities, I kept in touch with the various units to try to determine where the heck those Marines were. As each hour passed, I imagined increasingly worse scenarios that had befallen them. Maybe they had hit a kangaroo and been seriously injured, maybe their car had hit a tree, maybe . . . I didn't know.

While service members had certainly become disconnected from their units before, this was the first time I couldn't account for Marines under my command. I was trying not to freak out, focusing instead on Major Ryder's methodical approach to looking for them. He was concerned but not quite worried, as I was.

Finally, around 11:00 p.m., my Marines showed up at the base camp. Their Humvee had developed engine problems halfway out to the battlefield. Since none of them was a mechanic, they spent a good part of the day brainstorming how to get the engine running again. They discovered that they could drive the vehicle a short distance at low speed before having to turn it off to avoid overheating. So they spent the rest of the day attempting to return to base. I also learned that they did go into the field with a radio, but that the battery had died along the way.

I was so relieved to see them that I could have kissed them, but I didn't. While I'm sure they wouldn't have minded (I was the only woman they had seen in weeks), it wouldn't have been appropriate. Instead, I told them to get cleaned up and ready to go back out to cover the night attack from the colonel's position. I also promised that they'd get a break once they got back.

Once I realized that the three Marines were missing, Major Ryder pushed me into crisis operations mode. That didn't mean stopping everything I was doing to focus on finding the Marines, however. That's not practical or smart in most situations. Instead, I aviated— I continued to handle my primary responsibilities. Then I navigated: with the help and guidance of Major Ryder, I began running through all the possible ways to track down the Marines. I searched for a solution without interfering with my existing duties. And I communicated throughout the situation, keeping the sergeant major and the colonel informed of my progress, and asking other Marines for help in trying to locate them.

When you're in a crisis, don't panic and freeze—that won't solve anything. If you feel you're in over your head and don't know how to handle the crisis, seek counsel from someone with experience who can help you deal with the situation at hand.

The crisis was resolved within a matter of hours, with no negative impact on either the military exercise or the three Marines involved. And that's how I learned firsthand that leaders get through such situations successfully by aviating, navigating, and communicating. Courtney faced a crisis of her own while on duty in Washington, D.C., a few years ago. Fortunately, she, too, resolved the crisis without incident using this effective leadership principle.

SOME CRISES CALL FOR CREATIVITY

Courtney

My brief report of the night's activities read: "Flew 15 ceremonial flags over the Marine Corps War Memorial to commemorate the Fourth of July. One flag caused clips to become lodged in the statue. Problem was resolved in a safe, orderly manner." Yet that summary left out most of what had occurred the previous night as I served as duty officer at Marine Corps headquarters in Washington, D.C. The duty officer is the Marine who handles any problems that occur during the evening hours, after everyone else has gone home. Some nights I would have to break up a fight or bail Marines out of jail, but on the night of July 3, 1999, while I was on duty at the Pentagon, my experience was a little out of the ordinary.

One of the unique responsibilities of the Pentagon duty officer is the flying of ceremonial flags over the Marine Corps War Memorial. Better known as the Iwo Jima Memorial, the statue is an awe-inspiring tribute to the World War II flag-raising atop Mt. Surabachi. The 78-foot-tall bronze and granite memorial is truly breathtaking; it stands as a symbol of hope, promise, and victory. It captures the spirit of the Marine Corps motto: Semper Fidelis—Always Faithful. And to ensure that the memorial always reflects the spirit and sacrifice of the men and women of the Marine Corps, a 1961 presidential proclamation ordered that a flag fly over the War Memorial at all times. As duty officer, it was my responsibility to ensure that this order was fulfilled.

It was also my responsibility to fill requests from the American public for a flag that has flown over the memorial. It was my job to bring the requested flags down to the memorial, run them up the flagpole, render a proper salute, and then run them down to be boxed and sent to the individuals who requested them.

As one of the newest members of the unit, I was assigned to duty over the Fourth of July holiday. My duty began at 7:30 a.m. on July 3 and ended at 7:30 a.m. on July 4. When I arrived at the duty hut the morning of July 3, I noticed a larger-than-usual pile of flags to be flown over the war memorial. The officer heading off duty explained that typically there were more requests for flags that had been flown over the memorial on a patriotic holiday, such as the Fourth of July. He suggested that I complete the task as soon after midnight as possible, so as not to interfere with the planned Fourth of July activities that would begin early the next morning. As an area native, I knew how busy the war memorial would get the next day.

At the stroke of midnight that night, I drove to the memorial with a military policeman (MP) and a box of flags, ready to complete the flag flying as efficiently as possible. Since the young MP I was with was taller than I was, we agreed that he would climb the short ladder we had brought to reach the ropes at the bottom of the flagpole on top of the statue. My job was to stand on the ground and give each flag a proper salute as he raised and lowered them.

As he climbed to the top of the monument, I gazed around us at the skyline, struck by the sight of the Washington Monument against the clear sky, the majestic Lincoln Memorial, and the statue of the four Marines and one sailor that was next to me. I felt lucky to have the opportunity to see these sites during the quiet night, lit so brilliantly. Unfortunately, my luck was about to change.

Once the Marine reached the base of the flagpole, I handed him the first of the 15 flags to raise high for me to salute. Done. On to the next. We worked methodically. He raised the flag, I saluted it, and then he brought it down for proper boxing. The process worked flawlessly until the twelfth flag. The sound of a quick snap and a loud clang signaled that disaster had struck.

"Um, Ma'am. The clip is stuck at the top, and I can't pull it down," the Marine reported to me.

"Are you sure? Can you pull harder?" I asked, hoping that a sharp tug would correct the situation.

If it hadn't been so dark, I'm sure I would have caught the corporal rolling his eyes, as if to say, "Duh, Ma'am. Like I didn't try that already." Instead, he humored me by pulling the ropes again. I listened carefully for the hum of metal against the rope, the sound the clips make as they slide down the flagpole. Nothing. Again, he pulled. Again, nothing.

"Don't worry, Ma'am. I can climb up over the Marines, then climb up the flagpole and get the clip," the corporal reported. I quickly analyzed that option. Picturing the corporal falling to his death from the 78-foot flagpole, I vetoed it and asked him to climb down.

There I was, at a memorial to the world's most famous flag-raising. No flag was currently flying, the clips required to hold the flag were 78 feet in the air, and tomorrow was the busiest, most patriotic day of the year. What was normally a routine task had suddenly morphed into a full-blown crisis—one that was my responsibility to handle.

I ran through the situation in my mind. What would it take to deal with the problem? A big ladder, I decided. Who had a really big ladder? The fire department! Although I wasn't sure the local fire department would be willing to help, I thought the lack of a flag flying over an important memorial might be enough to get them out that night. I held my breath and called the Arlington County Fire Department.

I was immediately transferred to the station with a hook and ladder that was closest to the memorial. I pleaded my case to the shift supervisor, hoping that someone in his unit was a former Marine. Fortunately, the supervisor shared my sense of adventure and saw the potential training value for some of his rookie squad members. He told me he would have the truck out in 30 minutes. With a huge sigh of relief, I called the park police to alert them to the situation and to let them know why a fire truck would soon be entering the grounds. They approved and even asked to come watch.

The only other obstacle standing between me and the completion of my flag-raising duties was a decorative chain-link fence that runs around the perimeter of the perfectly manicured lawns surrounding the memorial. Seeing no other way to remove the fence, the corporal and I set about pulling up each of the fence posts, making way for the fire truck.

The fire truck backed up slowly, trying to minimize the damage to the lawn, but the lawn was a goner. As a very able fireman scaled the ladder and untangled the flag clip, I was already thinking ahead to how I was going to repair the landscaping. But our first task was to finish flying the remaining three flags. The heroes of the fire department stood by and watched as the corporal and I flew the last of the flags and then raised the large, ceremonial flag back into place. (Little more than two years later, the same fire department would be first on the scene at the Pentagon on September 11.)

As the fire truck pulled away and the morning sky was brightening, the corporal and I got to work on the lawn. We replaced all the fence posts and did our best to get the grass back into an attractive and upright position.

My report of the night's activities was accurate but bland, with no details of the drama of the night before.

As a leader, it was my responsibility to come up with a solution to the crisis I was facing. Figuring out how to deal with the tangled flag clips and get the flag flying over the memorial again was part of my job description, just as any leader focuses on problem solving in the face of a crisis. I couldn't just walk away and leave the situation for the next duty officer to deal with—I needed to overcome the problem before my shift was over. Yes, it was a nerve-wracking experience, but I led my way out of it. I aviated and navigated. I also communicated with the fire department and park police to keep everyone apprised of my activities, and then I reported on my mission's success in the logbook. That's what a leader does: remains calm, looks for solutions, implements them, and then moves on.

> Creative solutions often arise out of your ability to analyze crisis situations with an open mind. Aviating, navigating, and communicating will help keep your mind clear and open to possible solutions to your current predicament as you continue to take steps to resolve it.

It's sometimes more difficult to put this process into practice when you're dealing with a personal crisis, but doing so is equally critical. Fortunately, aviating, navigating, and communicating can also help you avoid crises altogether. You don't have to wait until you're embroiled in a crisis to begin using this approach. As soon as you can predict that major changes will occur in your work or personal life, you can maintain control by aviating, navigating, and communicating. That's exactly what Angie did not too long ago as she faced a number of significant changes in her personal life.

ACCEPT THAT CHANGE IS CONSTANT

Angie

A crisis can be a life-and-death situation, such as that involving my Marines in Australia, but it can also be a situation that makes you feel overwhelmed or that you're not sure how to handle—such as during times of extreme change. That's exactly what I faced in the fall of 2004.

I was working full-time as a pharmaceutical rep by day and spending the rest of my waking moments on Lead Star in the hopes that one day I could quit my day job and dedicate all my energy to the company. My husband and I had recently bought property in Michigan, where we hope to retire, and had withdrawn a big chunk of our savings account to make the down payment. We were going to have to scrimp for a while to pay for the property, but we were confident that with both our jobs, we could afford it.

Right after our real estate purchase, out of the blue, I was informed that my employer was realigning my sales territory and assigning me to a headquarters city 90 miles away. Though I was used to a lot of windshield time, this would add two hours to my daily commute. I would have to be on the road and away from my husband much more than I had expected, or wanted.

Just like that, I had a crisis. We'd assumed that we'd be able to quickly replenish our depleted savings account with the money from both our incomes, and now my job was going to change. Was I willing to accept the changes? Work/life balance is important to me, and these new job terms didn't seem to match what I was looking for. Could we afford it if I quit? How would we manage to cover our living expenses and our new mortgage?

I continued to report to work every morning while I surveyed my career options—I aviated. Once I had zeroed in on my priorities, which included a job that didn't require a 12-hours-a-day commitment, I began brainstorming both my options for generating an income and how my husband and I could survive on his income alone until Lead Star took off—I navigated. I pointed my career toward what I really wanted, which was to devote myself full-time to leadership consulting at Lead Star. Once I had made the choice, I communicated my resignation to my employer.

Despite having made the decision, I was still stressed about how we were going to make ends meet while Courtney and I got Lead Star up and running. Starting our company was one of the greatest professional risks I had ever taken, so when I was feeling a little "off" one day, I attributed this to nerves. But on the second day, when I couldn't shake my nausea, I decided to take a pregnancy test. Boy, was I stunned when I saw the little plus sign in the test window, indicating that I was expecting. This couldn't be true, I thought. So I ran out to buy a second test, the kind that has indicators that read "pregnant" or "not pregnant." I wanted to be sure. After the second test, I was sure. Yup, I was pregnant. My husband's reaction to the news was similar to mine: "How did that happen?"

Granted, the news wasn't totally unexpected, but it was still a shock. I was excited, scared, happy, nervous, and a million other emotions all at once. As Matt and I thought ahead to my due date, we realized that our baby would be born just about the time we were scheduled to move to Quantico, Virginia. How would I manage to quit my job, pour all my energy into starting a business, finish writing this book, put our house on the market and sell it, move to another state, and have a baby, all within a few short months? I was exhausted just imagining it. Logistically, it was overwhelming. I had no idea how I'd do it, but I fell back on my leadership training to figure it out.

Every day, I worked on Lead Star, took a step toward readying our home for the move, made sure I took care of myself and the baby, and kept a close eye on our finances, which were carefully budgeted—I aviated. I also navigated by working with Matt to prepare a timeline for everything that needed to happen in the coming months. Then we communicated—with our families, our friends, and, of course, Courtney, my business partner and friend extraordinaire. Although my maternity leave would cut into our travel schedule for a few months just when the business was really taking off, she was a true leader and assured me that we would make it work.

Judge Daniel Morgan arrived on June 4, followed shortly thereafter by our move to Virginia on June 28. Throughout the tumult, Courtney and I worked together to keep Lead Star business coming in and avoid any major disruption to the company. My mom traveled to North Carolina to help us with relocating and taking care of little Judge. The Marine Corps family network also did a tremendous job of supporting us, ensuring that our move would be as seamless as possible. With proper planning and constant communication, we made it through the crisis.

Careful planning and initiative help prevent crises from erupting. Anticipating change, rather than being overwhelmed by it, also helps to ensure that you always have several options for dealing with unexpected news and situations.

RESPONDING LIKE A LEADER

Virtually anything qualifies as a crisis if it hits you unexpectedly, adding new activities and responsibilities to your already harried life. A crisis can be as short-lived as a child being missing for five minutes at the mall, who is found by systematically retracing your steps and communicating the situation to nearby personnel, or as significant as being laid off from your job or discovering that you have a serious health condition that needs treatment. In many cases, you can't change the underlying situation (the thing that caused the crisis), but you can keep moving forward with your plans, adjusting and adapting them as needed to get beyond it. That's where the principle of aviating, navigating, and communicating comes in.

Leaders spend more time on problem solving, on progress, than on finger pointing and trying to figure out who or what to blame for a predicament. It often doesn't matter who is to blame—it's much more important to develop potential approaches to moving beyond the crisis, whether a long-term solution or a short-term panacea. The key is not to stop in your tracks, to shut down or become immobilized by a crisis. Getting caught up in the circumstances can only make the crisis worse and longer lasting. Finding a way out of the situation is much more constructive and useful. Aviate, navigate, and communicate your way out of a crisis.

CHAPTER SUMMARY POINTS

• Crises come in all shapes and sizes. If something is unexpected and overwhelming, it's a crisis. But crises are also surmountable if you remain calm and think through each step toward resolution.

• Take a deep breath. Keep your cool. Brainstorming plans and solutions to a crisis is easier when you're calm, as Angie learned when she dealt with missing Marines in a vast country or as Courtney learned when she had to come up with a solution to a stuck flag the day before Independence Day. Your brain has difficulty functioning when you're emotional and distressed.

• Aviate. Keep doing what you're doing while you assess the extent of the crisis. Gather information, but don't drop the ball. Angie kept tabs on all the efforts to locate her missing Marines, but she also continued to perform her normal job duties. She multitasked, adding one more responsibility—the safe return of her Marines—to her daily to-do list.

- Navigate. Analyze the information you have on the crisis to determine possible courses of action. Develop a strategy, an action plan to deal with the situation. Courtney quickly generated possible approaches to correcting the stuck flag clip and returning a flag to the top of the monument by reviewing her basic dilemma and then devising potential solutions to her predicament—the flag clip was stuck, and it was 78 feet in the air. Creativity based on the facts led to a solution.

- Communicate. Let others know what's going on as you work to develop your solution. Also, ask for help when you need it. As soon as Angie discovered that she was pregnant, she immediately shared her news with Courtney so that they could strategize how to alter her future consulting engagements during a brief maternity leave. Waiting to break the news would have made reworking the company's commitments difficult.

CHAPTER 7

COURAGE + INITIATIVE + PERSEVERANCE + INTEGRITY = SUCCESS

When you set a goal and achieve it, that's success. It doesn't really matter what the goal is, as long as you decide what you want, take steps to accomplish it, stick with it when the going gets tough, and remain true to yourself as you strive for it. Goals and objectives can be fairly simple, such as catching up on your overdue expense reports, or more challenging, like earning a college degree. They can be short-term or long-term, realistic or aspirational, easy or hard. They can also address different aspects of your life: work, home, school, family, health, spiritual, and financial are possible areas to consider. For instance, career-wise, you may aspire to be promoted to a certain level, or perhaps you want to own your own business one day. But work isn't everything, and setting personal objectives is to your advantage, too. Health targets, such as running two miles a day or switching to a low-cholesterol diet, are also smart. Saving money for a down payment on a house is a financial aim for many people, as is investing more time in their community or at their place of worship.

Goals are important because they lay out a path to accomplishing your dreams.

Without goals, there is no way to measure success. They are a yardstick by which we can gauge our progress toward our objective, toward success, however we define it.

Objectives help us stay focused on where we're headed. They help to prevent us from getting off the track or wasting time in a pursuit that doesn't move us closer to accomplishing our dream, such as quitting college to accept a full-time job when the desired goal is to earn a college degree. Goals give us a target to hit and keep our energies and efforts directed toward achieving success.

Setting goals is also the hallmark of a leader—someone who imagines where he or she wants to be in the future and then devises an action plan to get there, alone or with the help of the team. Leaders know that if they and their team are to achieve the success they desire, they need to have an end point in mind. Once they know the end point then they and their team can explore the various approaches for getting there.

Leaders also create opportunities for others to achieve their goals, first by finding out what those goals are, and then by supporting team members' efforts to reach them. However, we've heard from some of our workshop participants that while managers may *say* that they support their employees, in practice, it's not so clear-cut. Some managers, apparently, don't want to disrupt the team dynamic that is in place because it works. Or they feel that introducing change might damage their record of success. These managers aren't leaders, because leaders recognize that ambition is healthy and progress is good for everyone— they don't get in the way of their employees' goals.

Goal setting sounds so simple in theory, doesn't it? But in practice, it often isn't. The journey to success generally requires four steps, or phases; some of these can happen suddenly, but others may take weeks or even years.

The first step that is required in any journey to success is *courage*. Any change, even for the better, can be frightening. Whether you've been offered a significant promotion if you switch jobs or are considering adopting a child, it will take courage to pursue your opportunities. Courage is your ability to face your fears and uncertainty and move ahead anyway.

The second step is *initiative*—taking some action to move you toward your desired end result. Deciding to pursue an opportunity is a big step forward, but actually doing something will move you further down the path to success. It's been frustrating to hear how many women feel they don't have their manager's support in landing the promotion they're aiming for, but that lack of support doesn't mean that the promotion is out of reach; it just means that they need to take more initiative to demonstrate to others why the promotion should be theirs. Making a phone call to set up an appointment and visiting a Web site to gather information, for example, are two quick yet powerful actions you can take to get the ball rolling. Leaders set themselves apart from the rest of the world by acting on their dreams.

The third step is *perseverance*. Leaders have to expect obstacles, because there almost always are some, but must have the patience to persist. Pushing yourself toward your objective will take time, and the longer it takes, the more important it is that you remain dedicated to achieving your goal. Many people falter when the going gets tough, and some put aside their goals. As a leader, your ability to persevere may be challenged, but don't give up when you've come so far.

As you move closer to success, it's essential that you don't compromise your ethics or standards in order to achieve your goal. There have been too many stories in the news lately about corporate executives who took unethical shortcuts to success, such as misleading investors or fudging facts on their résumé. These people aren't leaders. Leaders have *integrity*—they always do the right thing, even when it's not the easiest or most popular course of action. They never have to wonder how they got where they are, because they know that they earned their success fair and square. Demonstrating your integrity also makes achieving your goals all the more gratifying.

In the Marine Corps, we learned about goal setting for success the day we signed up to become officers. Just because we wanted to become Marines didn't mean that we could. We had to earn that honor by demonstrating to our peers and our superiors that we deserved it. Through our experiences both as Marines and as professionals in the private sector, we realized that courage, initiative, perseverance, and integrity are four essential elements required to achieve success.

KEEP THE END RESULT IN MIND AT ALL TIMES

Angie

In high school, I was fairly successful. I got good grades, was a competitive athlete, and had many friends. But when I got to college, achieving success was more challenging. It was also lonelier. Unlike in high school, where my family and friends had regularly cheered me on and bolstered my self-confidence, in college I was on my own. When I doubted myself, there wasn't always someone there to reassure me. I realized that my success in the classroom and in ROTC was totally up to me, and that was scary. I frequently wondered, "What if I can't do it?" The answer was equally scary. So I tried not to think too much about failing.

During my freshman year, as I signed my application for the Marine Corps scholarship, I revealed to Major Samuel White, my superior, and Gunnery Sergeant Ed Robbins, his assistant, that I was afraid of what was to come. I admitted that I wasn't sure I could balance my schoolwork with ROTC demands or that I could survive the grueling 5 a.m. physical training sessions four days a week. I also wasn't convinced that I'd make it through Officer Candidate School (OCS), I told them, even though it was still nearly two years away.

"Angie, you have no idea what you're capable of," Major White and Gunny Robbins reassured me. "But you need to take each day at a time. Today, your objective is to sign the paperwork. You're going to experience a lot of fear and uncertainty along the way," they said. "But if you work past the fear, success is on the other side."

I was nearly overwhelmed by my fears, but I managed to push them aside. I was afraid of the hard work ahead, the physical pain I knew I'd feel, and the chance that after all the sacrifice, I still might not qualify to become an officer. Yet I signed the paperwork anyway—I focused on the immediate task and took the first step toward becoming a Marine officer.

Looking back, I see that Major White and Gunny Robbins helped me realize the courage I already had. I was afraid, but their encouragement prevented my fears from paralyzing me. I accomplished the task I needed to perform that day, signing the official agreement, rather than looking too far ahead at what was to come. I took one step forward. Then the next day I took another step, and so on, until I was immersed in the life of a Marine midshipman.

That life included morning training sessions that would wear out even the fittest officer candidate. I'd wake at 5:00 a.m., then head out to training at 5:30. The workout began with a three-mile run, followed by circuit training, where we did push-ups and sit-ups until our bodies gave out. Never before had I pushed my body beyond its limits—in high school, if I felt as if I was going to be sick while working out, I'd stop to give my body a rest. But in ROTC, stopping wasn't permitted, and puking was fully expected. Many mornings I'd even have difficulty blow-drying my hair after training because my arms ached so much. In the classroom, I often stood to prevent myself from falling asleep in my seat. I lived in a constant state of exhaustion.

Of course, like most college students, I was staying up late studying, then taking a break for pizza and a beer or two before hitting the sack around 1:00 a.m. But unlike many of my friends, I was getting up at 5:00 a.m., starting my classes at 8:00, and, once my classes were over for the day, heading off to work as an administrative assistant from 3:00 to 5:00 p.m., then returning to my apartment and repeating the routine the next day. After a couple of months of this, I realized that something in my schedule had to change if my body wasn't to give out. So I cut back my nightly carousing, revamped my schedule, and settled in for the long haul of school, work, and ROTC. Although I was still intent on having fun with my roommates, I recognized that in order to be successful as a Marine officer and a student, I needed to focus solely on those activities that would move me toward my goal. I had to take some personal initiative, even when I really wanted to be goofing off.

With less partying, I found that I had time to devote to more worthwhile pursuits, like volunteering for various ROTC activities. So I signed up to participate in everything from drill team, to military competitions, to color guard, and more. Although my initial reason for signing up for every activity under the sun was to improve my leadership skills, it was also a way for me to bolster what I perceived to be a weakness: my knowledge of the military. Viewing me as an overachiever, some of my fellow midshipmen made fun of me, calling me a die-hard "ROTC Nazi," which I strangely took as a compliment—I was doing everything I could to be successful as a Marine, and people were noticing. Their snide comments confirmed that I was on the path to success and helped me realize that the path would be lonely. In hindsight, I attribute my graduating as the midshipman battalion commander to the initiative I took early on with respect to ROTC. Taking the initiative early in any career can quickly set you apart from your peers.

Although I worked extremely hard to earn my place in the Corps, my journey to second lieutenant was equally challenging. The funny thing is, as hard as I had worked to be successful during the school year, when I went home for the summer, I began questioning whether all the effort was really worth it. I was sleeping more than I'd slept all year, working only one job during the day, and having nights and weekends free to hang out at the beach with my friends, and my reasons for joining the Marine Corps made less sense as the summer progressed. I was surrounded by people who didn't understand what the Corps had to offer, who'd remind me what I was giving up by making such a big commitment to the military, and it was hard not to start second-guessing my decision. My friends reminded me of my dream of being a teacher in northern Michigan, of how many years I'd be committed to the military, and how much more hard work I still had ahead of me. Seeing the Marine Corps through their eyes, I began to wonder what I was doing.

Toward the end of summer, my ambivalence about the Corps rose to the surface during an unexpected call from Gunny Robbins at 6:45 one morning. He wanted me to grab an "ink stick" to take some notes about upcoming midshipman activities on campus at the start of the new school year. As I yawned from the too-early hour, I told him that I wasn't sure I was going to return to the program and that I might decline my scholarship.

The objective of the call abruptly shifted. "Let me guess. You've been hanging around with friends who don't quite know what you're going through—who have no understanding of the military. Heck, some of them probably don't even like the military. Am I right?" He didn't wait for a response from me. "Then let me ask you this: What about Sad-Sack Sampson, Crazy Mitchell, D. J. Sanchez? What about those guys?"

The names he listed were Marine midshipmen in the class ahead of me. Gunny took sadistic pleasure in picking out names for all of us—mine was Judgment Day, a play on my maiden name of "Judge."

"What do you mean, Gunny?" I asked, puzzled by his question.

"I've had this same conversation with each one of them before they returned to school. Everyone has doubts. Everyone has fears.

But you're part of a team now, and Sampson, Mitchell, Sanchez, and I aren't going to let you walk away from this opportunity because you've spent your summer slacking off, having fun, and forgetting about your goals. I could let you quit, but I'm not going to," he told me. "Instead, I'm going to promise you that when you return—not if, but when—you're going to thank me for not letting you quit on yourself. Oh, you may not thank me tomorrow, or the next day, but you'll be thanking me eventually."

He was right. I did thank him—and let me thank him again now, publicly—for a pep talk that changed my life. He made it clear to me that I couldn't be a quitter—I didn't want to be a quitter! And he showed me the value of persistence and perseverance, all the while teaching me a lesson on integrity. Despite discouragement from some of my friends, who couldn't see how the Marine Corps was worth giving up years of my life for, I remained true to my plan, to my commitment, and to myself. I learned that I could be self-reliant and have the confidence to make a plan and stick to it until I had completed it. The Marine Corps, through the constant support of the major and gunny, allowed me to understand how to achieve the highest of goals. The day I pinned on my second lieutenant bars was one of the proudest days of my life. It was also the culmination of courage, initiative, perseverance, and integrity.

Any goal, no matter what size, can be achieved if it is tackled with courage, initiative, perseverance, and integrity. This isn't an overnight solution, but it's a methodical tactic that works.

While this formula fits well in the work world, it applies just as well to personal matters, as Courtney discovered while making the decision to become primary caregiver for her then-88-year-old grandmother, "Nana."

BELIEVING YOU CAN IS THE FIRST STEP TO SUCCESS

Courtney

I've always had a special relationship with my grandmother, so six years ago, when the opportunity arose for me to become her primary caregiver, I took it. From the Marine Corps, I knew that leadership was all about service to others, and I wanted to serve my grandmother, whom I love dearly. My mother had been taking care of her, living with her in my grandmother's home in suburban Virginia, but when my mom's doctor advised her against continuing as caregiver in order to preserve her own fragile health, I mustered my courage and stepped up to take over.

Like many women who assume this awesome responsibility, I believed in my heart that I could do it, but the how—how I was going to move all my belongings from my high-rise apartment into her home, how I was going to blend her scheduled doctor visits and my work requirements, how I was going to have a social life—was a different matter. I knew my life was about to change radically, but I wasn't exactly sure, going in, what that meant. So I focused on what I needed to do that day, which was simply to make the decision to assume the responsibility, and left the specifics of the arrangement to be worked out during the coming weeks and months. One step of courage got me started.

I took the initiative to ensure that Nana would have the best care possible, from me in her own home, but I soon discovered that initiative isn't just a one-time event. In Nana's case, I try to take initiative on an ongoing basis. That helps to keep our respective routines running smoothly and heads off many problems. During the last six years, Nana and I have both changed. In her case, she's progressed from a cane to a walker, to a walker with wheels, to occasional use of a wheelchair. With each change, I tried to anticipate what changes in her environment might be helpful, such as adding safety bars or modifying routines, and then took the initiative to make her more comfortable and safe, while remaining sensitive to her feelings about such adjustments.

Initiative is also critical to keeping the house running smoothly. I take a proactive role in ordering refills of her medications, making doctor's appointments, and coordinating weekly outings and activities to ensure that there are no schedule conflicts. I also synchronize family visits so that she has a steady stream of different guests throughout the week, and schedule magazines and TV shows to avoid a lull in entertainment. Once Nana has been taken care of, I can claim some time for myself.

Although my initial commitment was to care for Nana for a year, one year has turned into six, and Patrick and I have no plans to quit. We'll be here with Nana for the rest of her life. Sure, taking care of her can be challenging and frustrating, such as when she's sick or upset, or frustrated by the effect aging has on her body, but it's also extremely rewarding. Sticking with Nana, persevering even during the tough times, has shown me how to love so much more deeply, taught me to be a million times more patient, and given me the opportunity to see joy and delight through someone else's eyes.

During our time together, I've also seen the importance of integrity. As my grandmother's caregiver, I assist her in making many decisions, but I do my best to give her any and all information that I have and then let her make her own choices. I help her manage her finances, but I don't want or ask for control over her funds. I gather information about her health care, but I always involve her in her medical decisions, so that I can be true to what she wants, rather than what I or our family may prefer. I work hard to be a source of information for her, rather than a filter, and do my best to withhold my personal opinions unless she asks for them. The integrity I learned in the Corps has helped make me a professional success *and* helped strengthen my relationship with my grandmother.

Sure, initially I was nervous about making such a big commitment to my grandmother, but by using these four steps—the recipe for success—I was able to move forward. I've found that in situations where I need to make a choice that isn't easy or popular, falling back on these four steps helps tremendously. I've been able to be true to myself but also push beyond my comfort zone to do more than I might have thought myself capable of. These four steps allow me to envision what I want and then begin taking the steps needed to achieve it, which is exactly what I did during my first overseas tour.

> Whenever you feel overwhelmed by a goal, break it down into smaller steps that you can easily accomplish. Then complete the first one. Don't worry about Step 5 or Step 10; just focus on the first step. Then go to the second. Soon you'll be amazed at the progress you've made.

IF YOU CAN DREAM IT, YOU CAN DO IT

Courtney

The Marine Corps taught me that if you have a vision, you can make it a reality. When I joined the Marine Corps, one of my dreams was to serve my country overseas, so I requested an assignment anywhere in the world but the United States, and I got it. When the time came to leave for a one-year tour of duty in Okinawa, Japan, I was nervous about being so far from home, but also excited about the adventures to come.

On my arrival in Japan, I reported to the officer in charge, Major Steve Ricks. Major Ricks was an extraordinary leader, I quickly learned. He believed that if you could dream it, and if it would contribute to our mission as public affairs officers of promoting the stories of Marines everywhere, you should do it. He gave his team plenty of leeway to determine for themselves how they could best serve the Corps. One way he did that was by giving each Marine a broad title and a rather vague description of his or her responsibilities so that each of us could define how we could best do our job.

My title was "Distribution Officer," and I was responsible for communicating to the world what the "most forward deployed" Marines of the Third Marine Expeditionary Force were doing. Although my fellow lieutenants joked that my title meant that I was responsible for delivering the base newspaper and mailing some copies back home, I was actually quite pleased with it. I saw how wide-open my job duties could be and had big plans to make the most of my assignment. Instead of limiting my duties to what lieutenants typically did, I mustered the courage to think bigger than that.

During one of my early staff meetings with my team in Japan, I laid out my plans for my role as distribution officer. I had already called many of the units stationed around Japan and prepared a list of the many exercises and humanitarian operations they were involved in that could be covered. My plan was to make videos of Marines in action in remote spots and feed the material to television producers back in the United States to assist them in developing positive stories on the Marine Corps' work to air in major cities. To do that, I had prepared a list of potential deployments to Indonesia, Thailand, and mainland Japan, where the video footage would be shot.

The senior staff in the meeting thought that the approach was great but, unbeknownst to me, were skeptical that a brand-new second lieutenant could pull it off. In fact, they thought the idea was outrageous, but they gave me the go-ahead anyway, curious to see how I'd fare. Fortunately, Major Ricks truly believed in my abilities and gave me his full support as I coordinated Marine units and Air Force equipment to make the videos a reality. Some days my perseverance was severely tested, as some requests for personnel or materials were turned down. In those cases, I'd meet with the higher-ranking officers personally to plead my case. Eventually, the requests were approved. But even after I had the video footage in hand, I had to be persistent in trying to reach U.S. TV producers, who were in a time zone 13 hours behind us. I often worked late into the night to try to catch the producers at their desks and attempt to persuade them to run a Marine Corps story.

Even as I worked endless hours to make my initiative a success, I also had to stop and ask myself from time to time whether my efforts would truly benefit the Marine Corps, or if creating opportunities to travel the world was my higher priority. Keeping my integrity intact as I managed this large program was important to me. Shortly after returning from a deployment to Indonesia, my first trip, I got my answer. The video press releases I had created resulted in positive feature stories on the Corps in 23 U.S. markets, and many of the producers asked for more of the "positive military stories" I was developing. My confidence soared as the importance of my work was confirmed.

Now, each time I face a new opportunity or uncharted territory, the four-step process for success has become a routine. And that's the great thing about this recipe for success: once you display courage, take initiative, persevere through tough times, and maintain your integrity, the process starts to extend into other areas of your life. Not only will you be more successful at the individual projects or efforts you're focused on, but also your success in those will have a positive impact on the other roles you play.

> Leaders constantly set goals to help them achieve the life they want to live. They have vision. Challenge yourself to dream big, rather than settling for what others think you deserve. Set large goals.

SUCCESS STORIES HAVE A COMMON THEME

If you take a minute to reflect on what you consider to be the major successes in your life, we bet you'll see a pattern. In each instance, you'll probably be able to identify the moment that took the most courage, the action that required real initiative, the instances when you really wanted to quit but didn't, and some situations when you could have compromised your integrity but chose not to. Success stories have common threads.

Conversely, if you think about the areas of your life where you're struggling, you'll probably have little trouble picking out what's lacking. Perhaps you haven't yet found the courage to envision your life differently, or maybe you can picture how you want your life to be, but you haven't taken that all-important first step to make it happen—you lack initiative. For some of us, perseverance is the toughest part. You know what you need to do, and you've taken the first step, but the change you want is taking much longer than you expected, and you've reverted to some bad habits or even given up temporarily. Or maybe you tried to take a shortcut and compromised your integrity, and that's damaging your future success. White lies, selfishness, and other weaknesses can really interfere with success—we know because we've been there.

Here's your chance to start over with a clean slate—to be a successful leader in every aspect of your life.

What's your definition of success today? Where do you see yourself in five years? What about in five months? What do you need to do to get there? And what's holding you back from reaching your goal? Using these four steps, map out your path to success and take action. We know you can do it.

CHAPTER SUMMARY POINTS

• Success isn't magic, and it doesn't happen suddenly. It's the culmination of several steps—four, to be exact—that together lead you to the success you want. Small steps count, as long as they're headed in the right direction.

- The first step on your journey to success is courage, the ability to face your fears and uncertainty and move ahead. It's a willingness to change. Despite Angie's concern about what her Marine Corps future might hold and her anxiety about the hard work ahead, she focused on her immediate task: signing the papers to make her Marine Corps role official. That took courage.

- The second step is initiative—the first action step. Initiative is momentum of a sort: the desire to change becomes so strong that you take some action to get you moving in the right direction, whether it's joining a health club to get in shape or scheduling an appointment with your boss to discuss what you need to do to get promoted. Given the opportunity to define her own job, Courtney dreamed big. She imagined the difference she could make, and she took the initiative to carve out an important role. Then she proceeded to act on her goal, taking small steps to achieve her objective.

- The third step is perseverance. It's sticking with your course of action even when you start to wonder if it's doing any good. In many ways, this is the hardest step. Even when some of Angie's friends tried to dissuade her from joining the Corps, she persevered. She ignored their negativity and proceeded toward her goal of becoming an officer. She stuck with her plan, her goal.

- And the last step is integrity, which is remaining honest and ethical at all times. Taking shortcuts such as hurting someone else or telling white lies will hamper your success. Your success can happen only if you demonstrate integrity 24 hours a day; every moment you lack integrity keeps you that much further from success. Courtney's role as caregiver for her grandmother gives her influence over Nana's life, but she takes great care not to overstep any ethical boundaries. She is clear about what her role is and that the decision-making power rests with her grandmother. Stating up front what she will and won't do helps to solidify important ethical limits.

• Successful leaders approach every goal using this formula. Look at the career history of great leaders and you'll undoubtedly be able to see how each one combined courage, initiative, perseverance, and integrity to achieve success.

CHAPTER 8

DON'T CRY OVER SOMETHING THAT WON'T CRY OVER YOU

Stress is a natural part of every leader's life. Your ability to handle it may be tested at any time—when traffic is backed up for miles and your kids are screaming in their car seats, when you arrive at the wrong office building for a meeting that is to take place within minutes, or when you discover that you have lost your wallet. Truthfully, these are situations that might test even the most capable leader's ability to handle stress.

Men and women respond differently to stressful situations. When men get frustrated, they typically raise their voices or become uncommunicative. But when women get frustrated or angry, they're more likely to cry. No, not every woman cries in such situations, but more women than men respond to stress with tears.

When stressful situations arise, it's normal to feel that a good cry will provide a needed emotional release. However, tears are not the solution you're looking for if you're at work. Tears never resolve conflict, don't correct problems, and don't contribute to the accomplishment of your overall mission. Also, when women show signs of tearing up, it makes those around them (especially men) uncomfortable. What's worse, tears chip away at your command presence, or your ability to inspire confidence in others through your demeanor. They create a perception of weakness, demonstrating to your team that you don't have emotional resolve. Leaders do have emotional resolve, so tears will damage your professional reputation. Unfortunately, when women lose control of their emotions, this often suggests to their team that they have lost control of the situation (or, rather, that they have caved in to the stressful demands of the situation). Granted, that's not always what tears mean (in many cases, they are just a sign of fatigue), but they have negative connotations that women need to be more aware of. Maintaining your composure is necessary for preserving the respect and trust of your teammates.

We've heard many women say that it's OK to cry at work—they're just expressing themselves. While we're glad that these women are comfortable with themselves and their emotions, we don't think they recognize the impact that their crying has on others, and on their reputation. When a woman breaks down, she is forever branded as "the woman who cried at work." Her professional reputation is tarnished, and her ability to lead is significantly damaged. Tears don't inspire confidence in someone's skills and can severely limit that person's ability to lead others. Instead of serving as a useful catharsis, as some women argue crying is, tears at work generally only make things worse. Tears and work shouldn't mix.

If you tend to cry under pressure, stopping yourself from doing so may be quite challenging. You may have already tried biting your lip, curling your toes, or simply excusing yourself from the situation, only to discover that these coping mechanisms don't stop the tears from coming. We know it can be extremely hard to hold back tears when you're close to breaking down. But for the sake of your reputation and your team, it's important for you to gain a new perspective on crying. Break the pattern of becoming emotional and feeling the tears well up by not crying over something that won't cry over you.

You must begin to view your tears as a valuable commodity—you don't want to waste them on situations or people who don't deserve them. Once you logically recognize the fact that your jerk boss, whose temper has no limits, isn't going to cry over you, why should you cry over him? The same is true for that demanding client who has a habit of calling at the eleventh hour with a life-or-death issue. And your computer, which has once again caught a virus and shut down, doesn't know how to cry over you, either. So why waste your valuable tears crying over it? It's simply not worth it.

Controlling your emotions by suppressing or withholding tears will help you maintain your professional reputation. You'll also stay focused on the task before you. Tears are distracting and can detour you away from progress. Holding them back keeps you focused on your objective.

This doesn't mean that you should never cry, though. Tears aren't something to be feared. There is just a time and a place for them. Tears are best spent on people you care about and in situations where emotions are heightened, such as the birth of a child, a friend's wedding, your child's graduation, or a grandparent's funeral. Leaders have feelings, too. You shouldn't mask your emotions in personal situations where you are genuinely feeling compassion, empathy, or sympathy.

Our life in the Marine Corps was not without emotions. In fact, the Marine Corps certainly gave us plenty to cry about. From the painful workouts, to the incredibly stressful war games, to the unwavering insistence on success, there were lots of situations where we both had to work hard to fight back the tears. We were frequently exhausted, frustrated, and pushed to our emotional limit, but what made it possible for us to keep tears at bay was our newfound realization, compliments of the Corps, that some things didn't deserve our tears, nor would tears help us do what we needed to do.

Courtney learned this lesson firsthand from her rifle instructor at TBS as she struggled to learn how to shoot.

TEARS CAN BE A ROADBLOCK TO PROGRESS

Courtney

Before I entered the Marine Corps, I had never fired a gun. Heck, I had never touched even a small pistol, much less a high-powered rifle. But the Corps believes that it can teach anyone to shoot accurately in just two weeks. I believed that the Corps had its work cut out for it. I had no natural shooting ability whatsoever. I felt awkward handling weapons, and the intense rifle training sessions often left me exhausted and unable to focus on the mission at hand: becoming a qualified marksman with an M-16.

Every day my unit would head out to the massive firing range at 5:00 a.m., participate in a long day of target practice, and return 12 hours later, at 5:00 p.m. Over and over, we shot at targets at various distances, from 25 yards to 500 yards. Sometimes my bullets would hit the targets, but many times they would not. I know this because after I was done firing, I would hear over the loudspeaker, "Target 26, no impact, no idea," meaning that since the bullet hadn't hit the target, the scorekeeper had no way to record my shots.

It didn't take long for me to be singled out by the training staff as a student in need of some extra assistance. I was assigned my own personal rifle coach to help me improve. In the civilian world, having a personal trainer is a status symbol, but in the Marine Corps, such one-on-one attention suggested a deficiency; no one wanted a personal coach. Unfortunately, I didn't have a choice.

Every Marine is a rifleman—every Marine but me, I thought. As an officer, I put extra pressure on myself to become proficient with the rifle. I also felt the pressure to prove to my coach, my unit, and the Marine Corps that I was capable of succeeding at this task. The repeated failure was frustrating, but I knew I had to keep my emotions under control. The rifle range is a very dangerous place, with 200 Marines firing thousands of rounds each day, and even one misfire can be deadly. Strong emotions and live ammunition do not mix.

One particular morning, right before I had to take the qualifying exam with my M-16, I was at my wit's end, and my instructor could tell. He sensed that I was nervous and stressed about passing the test. "Ma'am, just take a moment and relax," he suggested.

"Thanks, corporal," I said, forcing a smile. "I hate to fail, and I just can't figure out why I'm such a terrible shot. I've never had so much trouble learning to do something."

Embarrassed by my poor performance, I felt a lump well up in my throat, which only made me madder. Here I was, a Marine Corps officer holding a loaded M-16, and I was about to cry. What a baby I am, I thought. I swallowed hard, fighting to keep from crying in front of my instructor.

"Ma'am, I can tell you from experience, tears won't help you hit the target," he said. That sure got my attention! Here was this big guy with a barrel chest and huge arms telling me that he had cried over target practice. "Yep, I used to be a terrible shot," he revealed, "and, yep, I let myself sulk, and I even shed a tear or two. But now I'm an expert shot, and I'm here teaching others to shoot. Anyone can learn to shoot an M-16. Right now, you're mad and you're disappointed. You need to take that energy and channel it toward the target. That rifle is never going to cry over you, and neither is the enemy. So take that anger and frustration and send it down range with the bullet. Don't waste your tears on things that won't cry over you."

What great advice! My frustration and tears were a waste of energy and were only serving as a roadblock to my progress. Once I was able to let go of my emotions on the rifle range, I actually began to hit the target. By the end of our training, I passed the test and became a Marine Corps Marksman. It wasn't expert status, but given where I had started, I felt as if I had earned a gold medal! Not only had I learned to shoot, but I had also learned a lot about myself and the value of composure during tough times.

I still reflect on my coach's words today. Looking back, I certainly remember him for his wisdom. His practical reasoning on how to control your emotions was invaluable. But I also remember him for his extreme bravery. It makes me smile to think that he had the courage to face an emotional woman who was near tears and about to boil over—something most men would fear. Add to the situation the fact that I also happened to be holding a loaded M-16 and you have one brave warrior.

> Tears get in the way of performance. Instead of wasting your valuable emotions on circumstances that won't cry over you, use your energy to seek solutions and improve your performance.

Angie also dealt with tears in the Marine Corps. But her experience was different. She had to convey my rifle coach's message to one of her Marines who was having trouble maintaining his composure. While he appreciated the advice, he may not have recognized how even one tearful episode affected his career.

TEARS CHANGE A PROFESSIONAL RELATIONSHIP

Angie

Nineteen-year-old Lance Corporal Benton had joined the Marine Corps for challenge and adventure, he told me, but his actions suggested otherwise. He seemed to me to spend more time arranging his busy social schedule than attending to his Marine Corps responsibilities, and his paycheck went almost entirely to pay for his two major assets—his new car and his cell phone. This wasn't the typical behavior of a responsible Marine Corps leader, but it was a little too soon to tell whether he could get serious about his new role. One thing was certain: Benton clearly enjoyed his independence.

In many ways, Benton reminded me of my younger brother: he was full of spunk and mischief, but a little too naïve and a little too girl crazy for his own good. Despite his youth and inexperience, I wanted to give Benton an opportunity to succeed. As an officer, I cared about my Marines and looked forward to watching them achieve professional success and earn promotions along the way. So when I talked to him on the job, I tried to impress upon him the amount of work that being a Marine would require. I hoped he would show a little more work ethic.

During one of our exchanges, he sounded surprised that he was being called upon to work harder, but reassured me that he wasn't afraid of the extra effort that would be needed. I wasn't convinced that he understood how demanding his schedule would be, but he had made it through Boot Camp and had earned the right to be there, so I gave him the benefit of the doubt.

Unfortunately, the next time we met to talk seriously was only a few weeks later, and it was for a disciplinary review. I knew from past experience with struggling Marines that Benton was already in trouble. In the few short weeks he'd been in Hawaii, Benton had failed to obey a direct order from his sergeant and had failed to complete an assignment for the base newspaper. I knew I had to take action quickly to shake him up and get him back on track, so I drafted a nonjudicial punishment (NJP) form. NJPs are a disciplinary tool designed mainly to serve as a type of warning, much as a formal letter in a corporate personnel file does.

Benton stood in front of my desk as I reviewed his wrongdoings and explained the required punishment. It was hard not to notice that he was having trouble controlling his emotions. When

I spotted the first tear rolling down his cheek, I stopped talking and asked him to step outside and go to the restroom to compose himself. Once he had his emotions under control, we would continue the discussion, I told him.

I was surprised by his crying. But I was puzzled, too. I'm not intimidating, I'm not scary, I wasn't yelling or berating him, so why was he having such a hard time controlling his emotions? Here I was, trying to intervene early to help him get his Marine Corps career back on track, and he was responding by demonstrating that he couldn't handle the pressure. Not a good sign, I thought to myself.

When Benton came back in, we continued our conversation, but I have to admit that I toned down some of the language I had planned to use for fear I'd see tears again. I knew it was incredibly embarrassing for him to show his emotions in front of me, and I wanted to help him hold on to his last bit of dignity. So I reassured him that the NJP wouldn't tarnish his record; sure, it might slow down his next promotion a little, but it wouldn't have a negative effect on his career. Yes, he had screwed up, but if he turned the situation around, the screw-up wouldn't be career-ending by any means.

I also pointed out that I thought he was displaying more emotion than the situation warranted. He had made a mistake. I, as his leader, was showing him how he had screwed up and counseling him on how to correct his behavior. I was doing my job. The punishment wasn't personal and shouldn't be taken personally. I still believed in his potential as a Marine, but I was disappointed in his professional behavior, which is what the NJP reflected, I told him. Then I repeated the lesson that Courtney had learned earlier: he shouldn't cry over something that wasn't going to cry over him. I reminded him again that his reprimand was part of my job as his leader, and I wasn't going to cry over him, nor should he cry over me—I wasn't worth his tears, I told him. He smiled at that bit of wisdom and thanked me for it.

You might think that one episode, one incident, involving tears would be easy to forget, but it wasn't. That meeting, and Benton's reaction to the confrontation about his mistakes, changed the dynamic of our relationship. It also changed the way I viewed him and the types of assignments I gave him.

I didn't trust him as much with the high-stress jobs after that. When he went to provide media coverage to other units, I was always concerned that he wouldn't be able to control his emotions—that he would break down, damaging his ability to do his job and causing himself embarrassment. I also found myself treating him with kid gloves when there was a need for any kind of confrontation. I had witnessed his tears one time too many and wanted to be sure I never had to witness them again.

Although women are usually the ones who are prone to crying and emotional outbursts, and men the ones who become uncomfortable, I was in the unusual position of understanding exactly how men feel. The importance of remaining emotionally in control was never clearer to me than after my experience with Lance Corporal Benton.

> Tears change the relationship between you and your colleagues or teammates. Crying in front of others creates uncomfortable situations and interferes with your ability to lead. Work on controlling your emotions so that your reputation as a leader isn't damaged.

Another experience, this time in the private sector, drove home how damaging crying can be to a career. Having been trained as a Marine Corps leader, I was shocked by the amount of emotion that was shown routinely in the corporate world.

TEARS CAN BE CAREER-ENDING

Angie

During my career as a pharmaceutical sales representative, I was quickly promoted to senior sales representative. Earning the senior position required attending a rigorous two-month training course in New York to improve my science knowledge and my selling skills. I was excited about the opportunity.

My classmates and I spent days studying the science material and then took tests to check our grasp of the information. Once the individual science tests were over, we had to pass a daylong exam that evaluated our science knowledge and selling skills simultaneously. If we passed the test we could jump right into selling and making money. If we failed the test, we'd face a performance review that could result in our having to retake the entire course or being terminated on the spot.

There were about 70 of us being trained that session, including Lindsay, a new hire, and me. Lindsay had previous sales experience, but none in the pharmaceutical industry, so she had a little catching up to do to match those of us who had already worked in the field. Because Lindsay and I had the same manager and were going to be teammates, we ended up being partners for some of the daily study sessions. I could tell right away that she was overwhelmed by the whole experience.

After our all-day training sessions, Lindsay and I would often get together in the evening to review the day's material. The first night, she came to my room with red eyes and a puffy face, like she had been crying. I was concerned, thinking that something was wrong at home or she'd gotten bad news of some kind. No, she told me, everything was fine with her family, but she was very stressed about passing the training; she wasn't sure she could do it.

Now, Lindsay was much smarter than I in the science arena—she had a biology degree; I had an English degree. She quickly grasped the material we were given. But she couldn't handle the stress of test taking and frequently broke down in tears during our daytime study sessions. It seemed to me that she was being a bit dramatic.

Having been in pharmaceutical sales for a little while, I knew that hardly anyone ever failed the tests or got fired—that was a line the company used to make sure its sales team worked hard during the training sessions and didn't slack off. We all took our training seriously and worked hard, but I knew there was no need for her to be overly concerned about passing. Everyone passed, I told her. It didn't seem to matter. Despite my reassurance that her chances of failing were almost nil, Lindsay couldn't hold it together. She would often break down crying, overwhelmed and stressed by the experience. Soon our colleagues were pulling me aside to discuss Lindsay's tears.

I was concerned about Lindsay's reputation as well, so I worked behind the scenes to help her understand the negative impact of her tears. A leader helps others as best he or she can, and I felt a duty to try to improve Lindsay's reputation, or at least to help her change her attitude about her tears. I took some time to talk with Lindsay about her emotional displays and the importance of controlling her tears. I gave her some tips for getting a handle on her crying before it began, but she didn't seem receptive to what I had to say. She explained to me that tears were just her way of expressing herself, and her crying wasn't going to interfere with her professional relationships.

Based on my previous experience in the industry, I knew that many of the customers we called on weren't necessarily going to treat her kindly, or with respect. How would she handle it? I'd found that many people don't hold sales representatives in high regard, and being treated poorly was almost a given. Seeing her cry certainly wouldn't improve anyone's professional view of the rest of us, either. Lindsay needed to learn to separate her emotions from her job responsibilities.

It wasn't surprising that only three months later, Lindsay was let go. She had made it through the training but was terminated shortly thereafter.

Not too long after I heard the news, I was on a sales call with my boss, Katie. Katie asked if I had ever witnessed Lindsay losing her composure at work. I told her that I had. Then I asked if that was the reason she had been let go. While Katie couldn't discuss the specifics of what led to Lindsay's firing, she said that she "had difficulty coaching Lindsay, and that is what ultimately led to her being fired."

A few days after that, Lindsay gave me a call. She admitted that she had broken down in tears a few times in front of Katie, but she couldn't believe that was part of the reason she was let go. Then she proceeded to bad-mouth Katie for several minutes, while I just let her ramble on.

She just didn't get it. If she couldn't be trusted to control her emotions in front of her manager, how could the company trust her to be completely professional in front of its valued customers? Our company was dependent on its pharmaceutical representatives to help it sell its products, service its customers, and reach its sales goals. Tears would damage the company's reputation and its ability to sell its products. The company simply couldn't afford to have someone like Lindsay representing it.

If only Lindsay had recognized how damaging her tears were, her professional career could have taken a different course. Instead, she considered her tears acceptable and didn't recognize that they were a weakness. Tears can't be ignored.

Crying at work, even once, will have a long-lasting impact on your career. You risk damaging or curtailing your professional progress if you're unable to get control of your emotions. Once the damage has been done, overcoming it will require extra effort.

If tears have become routine in particular situations, you need to take a look at what's behind them. Tears are a signal that something is wrong. If you have to work too hard to fight back your emotions, your tears are probably a red flag that you have a problem. Maybe you work in a hostile environment, maybe something is wrong in your personal life and it's spilling over into your professional role, or maybe you're overextending yourself. If so, let your tears be an indicator that you need to take action.

TEARS SIGNAL THAT A CHANGE IS NEEDED

Courtney

I'm a confident person and, like many women I know, generally face new situations with a "bring it on" attitude. As women, we can handle a lot at once, but there comes a point at which we hit our limit. I hit mine a few months after 9/11, and it was tears that warned me that I needed to make some changes in my life.

After 9/11, I was called back to active duty in the Marine Corps—a jolting event that ultimately required that Nana and I move from the Washington, D.C., area to Norfolk, Virginia, a distance of several hundred miles, so that I could become part of the new Homeland Security team at Joint Forces Command. At the time I was attending law school, and I wanted to find a way to continue my studies while also serving in the Corps so that I wouldn't have to start back at square one after completing my service.

My commanding officer was very much aware of how the lives of the reservists new to his unit had been disrupted and was willing to work with us to make our transition back to active duty as smooth as possible. My generation had never faced a recall and many thought of the reserves as something we did on the weekend to stay involved in the military we loved; we never really believed that we'd be needed to augment active-duty troops. Then terrorists attacked and we were asked to put our uniforms back on.

There were a variety of positions available in the unit I was assigned to, including overnight work. I quickly volunteered for these duties, despite the fact that they were considered less desirable, because I thought that if I worked the night shift, I'd be able to continue my studies at William and Mary's law school, which was about an hour away from the base. My commanding officer was delighted to have a volunteer for the night shift and allowed me to continue my studies during my off hours. He cautioned me that I was taking on quite a bit, but as long as I performed at work, he would certainly support me, he told me.

So I began my round-the-clock schedule. I'd work the overnight shift, sleep for an hour or two, drive to campus, attend classes, drive home, take care of Nana, do my homework and reading assignments, sleep for another hour or two, and then head to work. Except for the fact that I was getting only a few hours of sleep, everything went fairly well the first few months.

About six months into my routine, however, I began to notice tears welling up for no apparent reason—beyond sheer fatigue, of course. Any confrontation, argument, or upsetting news became a reason for tears to flow. Because I'm a person who rarely cries, I knew immediately that my tears were a warning sign. I was extremely stressed and overtired, and my life lacked any semblance of balance. I'd taken on too much.

At first I felt that I was stuck. I couldn't quit the Marine Corps— I was legally required to report each night. I didn't want to quit law school, and I didn't want Nana to suffer because I was too exhausted to care for her properly or give her the attention she deserved. I had to channel my emotions into coming up with a solution. The tears I was shedding weren't getting me anywhere. The Marine Corps wasn't going to cry over me; my big, heavy law books never shed a tear, either. As a leader, I knew I had to be cautious about the emotions I was displaying—they weren't going to help me achieve my goals.

When I took a step back, I started to see what I really needed: I needed more sleep, and I needed to be more efficient. So at the start of the next semester, I chose almost exclusively classes that met on Tuesdays and Thursdays, reducing the number of days each week that I had to commute to Williamsburg to William and Mary. Then I asked a friend at law school for help—a place to sleep. With a bed available near campus, I could head to school right after my night shift ended at 3:00 a.m., avoiding any rush-hour traffic. Then I'd be able to sleep for five hours straight in her guest room, have only a five-minute drive to class, and head home after classes were over. Days when I had classes were certainly long, but stacking the majority of my classes on two days helped bring balance to the rest of my week and allowed me to be more available for my grandmother.

The tears and raw emotions were a sign that my life was running me ragged—that adjustments were needed. I knew that the schedule I was keeping wasn't ideal, but it was the only way I could see, at the time, to make all my roles work and keep my commitments.

I learned in the Marine Corps that while I can do anything, I can't do everything. Women do an amazing job of taking on additional responsibilities, generally without relieving themselves of existing ones. We just keep adding to what's on our plate. Sometimes we do it because we have to, and sometimes we do it because we want to. But eventually our overcommitting catches up to us. When it does, tears are often an early warning sign that changes are needed—that we've hit our limit.

If you ignore the tears, the balance that you desperately need will become even further out of reach. Instead, you need to acknowledge that the tears you're shedding are being wasted on situations or people who won't cry over you. Once you accept that your valuable emotions and tears are being misdirected, you'll be better able to look for solutions and to make needed changes.

After a year and a half of the combined night shift/law school responsibilities, I graduated from law school. The same month I earned my law degree, I was released from active duty. The journey had been tough, but I made it because I took notice of tears that sprang from nowhere without warning. My emotions alerted me that change was needed, allowing me to make adjustments and still stay on track to earn my degree. The schedule I was keeping was unrealistic in the long term, but with discipline and determination, it was a short-term solution.

> Let your tears be a warning sign of problem areas in your life that need to be addressed. Strong emotions signal that something is wrong. Take some time to assess areas that may be a source of frustration or disappointment so that you can begin to make improvements.

LEADING WITHOUT TEARS

Leaders don't cry in front of their team over issues that will never cry over them. However, there are times when showing emotion at work may be appropriate, such as when you or a colleague experiences a personal tragedy. Not showing emotion in such situations would actually be rather heartless. Work-related issues, on the other hand, are not worthy of a leader's tears.

Fortunately, the more confidence you have in yourself and your abilities, the less you're apt to cry. When you know you can handle any situation that comes along—and you can—you won't have time to waste on tears or breakdowns. You'll be more focused on making progress or resolving the situation than on letting your emotions get away from you.

The leadership principle "Don't cry over something that won't cry over you" will help you carefully choose the situations in which you share such a personal emotion as crying. And most situations just aren't worth it. Instead, work hard on fighting back tears, even when you would normally let them spill, and regaining your composure so that others see you for the true leader you are. Don't let tears get in the way of your success.

CHAPTER SUMMARY POINTS

- Women often view crying as an innately feminine reaction to stress and believe that others understand. The truth is, they don't understand. Crying makes men (and many women) uncomfortable and changes their perception of the person—man or woman— who cries.

- Women who cry at work are generally viewed as more emotional, less capable, and less professional than those who are able to remain unemotional on the job. Crying can be a serious deterrent to career progress, as Angie witnessed firsthand with her colleague Lindsay. Tears cost Lindsay her manager's confidence and, ultimately, her job.

- Holding back tears and remaining composed takes work, but the effort to keep yourself together is well worth it in the professional world. When you feel tears welling up, ask yourself if you are about to cry over someone or something that won't cry over you. If you are, stop! If that's not possible, excuse yourself and get your emotions under control, as Angie directed Lance Corporal Benton to do during their discussion. His tears were uncomfortable for both of them.

- Tears are appropriate with those you care about —people with whom you share an emotional connection. They shouldn't be wasted on people or situations that don't reciprocate that emotional bond. Courtney's frustration with her inability to fire her weapon nearly led her to tears, until her instructor pointed out that her M-16 wasn't going to shed tears over the situation. Instead, she transformed that emotion into energy aimed at the target.

CHAPTER 9

SAY YOU'RE SORRY ONLY WHEN YOU'RE AT FAULT

Women probably say "I'm sorry" more than any other phrase in the English language. (Men also use the phrase, but far less often; we'll discuss this later in the chapter.) They seem to say it more than "thank you," more than "please," and possibly even more than "no." Like the phrase "you know," "I'm sorry" has become so common that it's merely filler in most conversations.

Instead of serving as an apology, as it was originally intended, "I'm sorry" has morphed into a versatile catchall phrase that is applied in a number of situations. It is used to head off confrontation, to appease others, to smooth over rough relationships, or to wrap up an argument, among other reasons. Think about the last time you said "I'm sorry"— did you really mean to apologize, or did you use it to sidestep a conflict or to downgrade simmering tensions?

Some women begin conversations with "I'm sorry," as in "I'm sorry to bother you" or "I'm sorry to interrupt, but our client is here," even when the phrase really has no place in the discussion. "I'm sorry" isn't a synonym for "excuse me" or "pardon me," although some women seem to believe it is. The phrase is significantly overused, and saying it regularly damages its powerful meaning. If you mean "excuse me," say "excuse me," not "I'm sorry."

Leaders say they're sorry only when they're at fault. They use the phrase to express regret or sorrow for the role they played in a situation or problem, such as making careless errors in expense reports or mishandling an unsatisfied customer. It is an acknowledgment of responsibility, not an excuse for poor performance. When used appropriately, it is said infrequently and sparingly. As a result, it also comes across as being more sincere.

We find it interesting that this leadership principle never fails to generate conversation and animated discussion. Many women argue that "I'm sorry" isn't as troublesome as we say it is. They believe it expresses empathy for someone else's situation. However, we believe there are clearer ways to communicate empathy than using an apology.

Overapologizing weakens a leader's reputation and damages his or her credibility. Picture a second lieutenant on the battlefield preparing to send her troops up a hill to attack an enemy force. She certainly doesn't precede her order with "I'm sorry," as in, "I'm sorry for sending you up the hill to put your lives on the line." Doing so would compromise her role as leader and would certainly damage her standing. Stressful, dangerous times are exactly when a leader's strength must be evident, not overshadowed by weak apologies. There are times and places for apologies, but leaders know that those situations are few and far between.

If you are truly sorry for something that you did, then an apology is in order. But don't apologize repeatedly for a single mistake or error—it rekindles bad feelings and suggests that you may have a victim mentality. Don't dwell on the situation or remind others of it; move on and forget about it. Spend more time suggesting solutions or ways to correct the error than apologizing for your role in causing the problem. Your focus should be on progress, on the future, not on past mistakes.

When you find yourself using the phrase "I'm sorry" frequently in your daily life, it may be a warning sign that you are overcommitting and underperforming. If commitments you've made routinely don't go as planned—if you regularly cancel client lunches or skip your weekly Friday night out with the girls—you may need to step back and look at your priorities. Maybe you're trying to do too much. You shouldn't need to apologize regularly.

Or maybe you're accepting responsibility for things you had nothing to do with out of guilt; guilt and apologies go hand in hand. Women often feel guilty for not doing enough or wish that they could do more, and apologize to make up for their perceived lack of action. For example, suppose your friend asks you to help her move over the weekend and it conflicts with your long-standing vacation plans, or suppose you just don't have the time to join the PTA at your child's school. You'd like to do more, but sometimes you can't. When you notice yourself apologizing quite a bit, you should examine your priorities: are you living the life you want? You need to accept responsibility for the choices you make and strive to make better ones if you discover that your priorities aren't aligned, or if they change. But don't apologize for those priorities.

Angie's priorities were certainly in alignment during her tour in Hawaii, but when an interesting situation arose during an Aloha Friday—essentially, Friday afternoon—she found herself apologizing as if she were somehow at fault.

UNNECESSARY APOLOGIES LEAD TO MISPLACED BLAME

Angie

Early in my tour as a public affairs officer in Hawaii, I encountered a bizarre situation for which not even Marine Corps training could have prepared me: a 20-foot-long dead sperm whale washed ashore on one of the beaches on the base, and my boss gave me the responsibility for marshaling the resources to deal with the situation.

As a Michigan native, I knew the protocol for handling dead deer on the highway—you call the cops and they get the job done. Dealing with a dead whale on a Hawaiian beach, however, is a little more intricate. Environmental issues, such as beached whales, are especially sensitive in Hawaii, and even more so when a military installation is involved. Immediately, I began fielding calls from the media and environmental groups that were interested in learning about the whale. In between taking those calls, I was also making calls to various Marine leaders to cordon off the area, help haul the carcass back out to sea, and let everyone in my chain of command know about the situation. What made the situation more challenging, however, was that it was Friday afternoon, when work comes to a halt in Hawaii and most senior officers head to the links to play golf.

I knew that asking them to return to base would be an irritation, an imposition, and as I placed calls to the officers, I anticipated how annoyed they would be to get my call. After all, I knew how I felt when I was called back to work after my weekend began. Feeling guilty for interrupting their game, I started the conversations something like this: "Lieutenant Colonel Jones, I'm sorry to bother you but there's a dead whale on Orange Beach," "Lieutenant Colonel Alexander, I'm sorry to bother you, but you need to come back to work to help handle this whale," and "Major Davis, yes, there is a dead whale, I'm sorry."

About halfway through the list of people I needed to call back on base, my boss interrupted me. Before he had even said a word, I could tell by his stern look that he was about to tell me something serious. I expected to hear that the situation was worse than had originally been communicated to me. Were there two whales? Was the public accusing the Marine Corps of foul play in the dead whale scenario? Was this situation going to play out over the entire weekend, disrupting my weekend plans? I braced myself for bad news. Instead of providing a barrage of information he asked a surprising question.

"Lieutenant, did you kill the whale?"

Confused, and thinking I must not have heard him correctly, I asked, "What, sir?"

"Lieutenant, did *you* kill the whale?" he asked again.

I was completely caught off guard, thinking that he must be crazy. "I'm sorry, sir, I don't get what you're saying. How could I have killed the whale? I've been in my office all afternoon."

"Well, Angie, I've been listening to you call everyone and their brother, apologizing for the dead whale on the beach, and I'm curious if you were in any way involved in the whale's death," he replied.

Now, Major Mark Rosa was normally a pretty laid-back guy, but he seemed to be particularly serious, so I knew he was trying to make a point. But he had caught me off guard and confused me with his question. Was I in trouble? Did he seriously think that I had something to do with the whale, I wondered? His question struck me as odd. Curious but stumped, I told him again, "No, sir, I didn't kill the whale. What do you mean?"

"Lieutenant, stop apologizing," he told me. "Stop saying you're sorry about the dead whale. Stop saying you're sorry that you're asking people to do their job. Nobody wants your apology; they just want to know what to do and when to do it. Do you get it?"

I did get it, sort of. I understood that he was trying to discourage me from apologizing for something that wasn't my fault, but it seemed like he was going a little overboard with his message. Why he was so bothered by my apologies didn't dawn on me until a few days later, when I had had a chance to think about it. Then it occurred to me that I was one of the few women he had worked with in the Marine Corps; he was used to the authoritative tone men are more prone to use in the workplace.

When most men talk, they don't apologize, which is why my apologies annoyed Major Rosa. He saw my apologies as unnecessary and unproductive, and interpreted them as a sign of weakness. I could see his point. Once I understood his reasoning, I worked hard to eliminate "I'm sorry" from my vocabulary.

Since then, I've continued to try to replace "I'm sorry" with phrases that more accurately reflect what I mean. For instance, if I'm going to interrupt someone, I'll say, "Excuse me." In some cases, "How can I help?" is more to the point when offering sympathy for an unfortunate situation; "I'm sorry" isn't appropriate unless I had something to do with a colleague losing his job or a friend breaking up with her boyfriend, for example. And if I'm feeling angry or upset, I don't apologize for having those feelings.

But I do have to keep myself from using "I'm sorry" to bow out of an argument rather than resolve the conflict. I've found that saying "I'm sorry" doesn't solve the problem; it just prolongs it and can even make it worse.

> Don't apologize for circumstances over which you had no control. Overapologizing can break down your command presence and chip away at the credibility you've worked so hard to earn.

APOLOGIES SIDESTEP CONFRONTATION BUT DON'T ADDRESS THE ISSUE

Angie

My husband, Matt, and I have a great, open, and honest relationship. We work hard at communicating. Sure, when we were first married we had typical couple arguments: "Why can't you put the seat down?" "Do I have to cook dinner every night?" Or "Why can't you just roll the tube of toothpaste from the bottom?!" We discussed our positions on these issues passionately, as insignificant as they were, until we worked through them.

But I started to notice that on more serious disagreements, such as those about money, our future, how many children we were going to have, and where we were going to live, I wasn't as passionate about defending my position. In fact, whenever we got into a heated discussion where we had opposing views, I tried to end the uncomfortable exchange with an "I'm sorry." I might say, "I'm sorry, I shouldn't have started this conversation," or "I'm sorry, but this is how I see it," as a way of firing a parting shot and walking away. Anything to avoid continued discussion, really.

I'm a peacemaker. I hate conflict and don't like to argue, so heated discussions with the person I love are really uncomfortable. My solution was to end the fight as soon as possible. However, I began to notice that we were fighting more and more over the same issues. I don't know how many times we argued about where we were going to invest our money, or how we were going to be able to afford a home in Los Angeles, where we were living at the time, but these things came up a lot. Because we never came to an agreement on a touchy subject or resolved things the first time around, we were doomed to repeat the same arguments over and over again. It was like the movie *Groundhog Day*, and just as draining.

I realized that when Matt and I reached a point in an argument (pretty much any argument) where it was obvious that we disagreed, instead of focusing on how to reach a compromise, I would bow out of the fight by saying "I'm sorry." Although my intention was merely to duck a confrontation—in effect, to table the discussion—Matt interpreted my apology as meaning that I had accepted his position. He thought I was telling him that the argument was my fault and that we could have avoided it if I hadn't voiced my opinion and pushed the issue. And the next time the subject came up, we'd have another round of fighting because he assumed that we had come to an agreement when we really hadn't.

Once I saw this pattern, I made a conscious effort to keep the discussions going, rather than avoiding them. I worked hard to make sure that I expressed all of my thoughts and opinions and that I carefully listened to and considered his position. Since I stopped apologizing, we've made a lot of progress. Sure, there have been plenty of uncomfortable moments (there still are from time to time), but we've managed to work through difficult issues successfully by tackling them head on. I also feel more satisfied with our relationship because we communicate as equals.

Part of that success is due to my confidence in my point of view. I find that the more sure I am of my position, the more comfortable I am expressing my opinion, and the less I need to use apologies to avoid contentious dialogue. I've seen some of the best solutions come out of the biggest disagreements. Although uncomfortable at times, confrontation is better dealt with than avoided. And that starts by not using apologies.

Don't use apologies to smooth over difficult situations or relationship impasses. Having the courage to face tough issues will help you resolve them and can make relationships stronger. Sidestepping issues with an apology will only allow them to simmer and worsen.

Although women are especially likely to overuse "I'm sorry," they're by no means alone. Men certainly use it, too. Courtney witnessed firsthand the impact that "I'm sorry" had when it was used by two men under her command.

THE MORE YOU APOLOGIZE, THE LOWER YOUR CREDIBILITY WILL BE

Courtney

Maybe because men rarely say "I'm sorry," when Sergeant Reynolds said it all the time, I noticed it. He apologized profusely for situations in an attempt to manipulate those around him. When he was late for work, for example, he would apologize and launch into a lengthy explanation of how his six-year-old daughter just wouldn't cooperate in getting dressed for school and he had to wait for her since it was his responsibility to drive her to school, and how sorry he was that she had made him late again. Or he'd miss a deadline and go overboard in apologizing for his tardiness. It didn't take me long to see that he was routinely apologizing for his lack of performance.

Once, after failing another fitness test, Sergeant Reynolds came to apologize for letting me down. "Don't be sorry you let me down, Sergeant," I told him. "I'm concerned that your poor performance will keep you from being promoted."

Although he tried to blame his underperformance on others— his daughter, his coworkers, his wife—it was clear to me that his apologies signaled his unwillingness to take responsibility for himself. As a result, he missed out on some valuable career opportunities; if he couldn't handle the rigors of everyday work, I certainly couldn't trust him with more responsibility. Because I didn't think he could work independently, for instance, I didn't submit his name as a candidate for a very desirable deployment to Hong Kong. His apologies damaged his career growth by damaging my confidence in his abilities.

In contrast, there was Corporal Nguyen. Corporal Nguyen was an outstanding Marine. He constantly looked for opportunities to provide additional assistance beyond his normal duties, which he performed well. His work ethic and no excuses attitude earned him a positive reputation, and I felt confident of his abilities and character. But, like everyone else, he wasn't perfect.

One time during a deployment, he lost a key piece of equipment—a camera tripod worth close to $3,000. Now, the Marine Corps keeps meticulous records on every single piece of equipment in its care. Losing gear is very serious. At The Basic School, if we lost a piece of equipment, it wasn't uncommon for an entire platoon of 50 people to be forced to spend hours scouring the woods for a $10 gear bag. So imagine the repercussions of losing something worth 30 times that amount—it wasn't pretty.

Recognizing the seriousness of the situation, Corporal Nguyen came forward immediately to tell me the bad news and to offer a simple apology. He didn't ramble on with excuses or try to put the blame on someone else, even though there were many others, such as the embark crew or the baggage handlers on the runway, who were more culpable than he. He accepted personal responsibility and expressed remorse, telling me: "The tripod we used on our deployment is lost; it's my fault, and I'm sorry." His heartfelt but brief apology impressed me.

As an officer, I was responsible for everything that my unit did and failed to do, so ultimately the loss of the tripod was my responsibility. But knowing that the loss was out of the ordinary for Corporal Nguyen made it much easier to explain the situation and complete the reams of paperwork to account for it. I also had a lot of discretion in disciplining a Marine who loses gear. In Corporal Nguyen's case, I didn't feel the need to put an official letter of reprimand in his personnel file—his remorse and acceptance of responsibility demonstrated his understanding of how serious the situation was. However, I did take the opportunity to have a serious discussion with him about the importance of keeping track of Marine Corps property. I chose the lightest sanction possible because of his credibility. As a result, this incident had no impact on his performance record. Had it been Sergeant Reynolds who had lost the tripod, I would have been much harsher with my sanctions.

Corporal Nguyen felt guilty for his actual involvement in the loss, which gave him credibility in my eyes. Interestingly, women often feel guilty for situations in which they have little or no involvement or responsibility. They lose sight of where their responsibility begins and ends, which may be why "I'm sorry" comes much more easily, and more frequently, to them.

> Apologies aren't a substitute for performance, and they can't reverse damage that has already been done. Frequent apologies compromise your credibility as a leader by suggesting that your underperformance is the norm rather than the exception.

That's not to say I haven't experienced misplaced guilt, however. I have, generally in situations involving friends and family.

YOU CAN'T HELP PEOPLE
WHO WON'T HELP THEMSELVES

Courtney

I normally don't mix money and friendship, but when my friend Kristina approached me in early 2003 and asked to borrow $1,500 to cover debts she couldn't currently pay, I agreed. It was a significant sum of money to lend, but she was a friend and I wanted to help her. When she asked to borrow money again two years later, however, I had to say no. "I'm sorry, I can't help you this time," I told her. Then I caught myself. Why was I feeling guilty? Why was I apologizing? Her poor financial situation wasn't my doing. In fact, I had already tried to help.

The first time Kristina asked me for money, I gave it to her on one condition: that she allow me to review her finances so that together we could create a budget for her to follow. I've always been interested in personal finance and meticulous about my own budgeting, so I truly felt that I could help her work through her situation. She had nowhere else to go, was down to her last dollar, and seemed to want to get out of the cycle of overspending she had gotten into, so she agreed. I was confident that I could show her the error of her ways and give her a foolproof plan for getting back on her feet.

As I went carefully through her finances, I saw that she was earning good money; she was simply spending more than she was making. She had frequent lavish dinners out, bought designer clothes, and gave expensive gifts to friends, with the result that it was tough for her to pay her mortgage and utilities at the end of the month. She could see what she was doing but couldn't break the pattern.

We spent hours analyzing where her money was going and establishing budgets for every aspect of her life to ensure that she could keep her spending under control and work her way out of debt. She committed to sticking to the plan, and I believed she was on the road to recovery. Then I was invited to a swanky party at her house, and I knew that she'd gone off course.

She was throwing a big blowout party—a catered affair, apparently—which definitely wasn't in her budget. I couldn't imagine that she'd saved enough in a few months to have extra money to spend on an expensive party, but I kept my mouth shut. It wasn't my money, and I had to stay out of it. When she began hinting that she was behind in her credit card payments, I felt sorry for her—not sorry enough to give her more money, but disappointed that she couldn't follow the budget I had so carefully developed for her. And if she couldn't stick with that plan, then I couldn't support her continued overspending. I sympathized with her, but I drew the line at throwing good money after bad.

Despite my irritation, I still felt guilty for not giving her more money when I could have. But I tried hard not to apologize when I turned down her requests for help. I reminded myself that I had done everything I could to improve her finances, and she just wasn't willing to make the needed changes. But that was her fault, not mine, and I shouldn't accept responsibility for it.

> Don't feel guilty or say you're sorry for your inability to help people. Continuously helping people who aren't making an effort to change is called "enabling" behavior, and there is no reason that you, as a leader, should engage in it.

Of course, it's harder not to feel guilty when personal relationships are involved, but refraining from unnecessary apologies in your professional life is especially wise. At work, "I'm sorry" puts the speaker in a position of weakness. Angie saw this repeatedly during her work as a pharmaceutical sales rep.

SELF-CONFIDENCE IS AN ANTIDOTE FOR "I'M SORRY"

Angie

As I grew more aware of how the phrase "I'm sorry" hindered my performance, I also recognized how others' apologies affected their leadership abilities.

During my time as a sales representative, I saw my colleagues lose credibility with their clients through their abundant and unnecessary apologies. In business, customers are always in a position of strength, but that doesn't mean that vendors and salespeople should be subservient or meek when approaching them. I was astounded at how many of the female sales reps around me became submissive when interacting with our doctor clients.

As a drug rep, part of my job was to give doctors samples of our products to use and to give to their patients, in hopes that they would like the products and prescribe them. Each time I stopped by to see a doctor, I would give out hundreds or even thousands of dollars worth of free samples. From my perspective, I had something of value to offer. I worked for a great company with great products. In exchange for a few minutes of the doctor's time, I would offer product samples. The catch was that the doctor had to physically sign a document indicating acceptance of the samples, in accordance with FDA regulations. Some of my colleagues saw asking the doctor for a signature as an imposition, however.

Consequently, they would begin their discussions with, "Sorry for taking your time" or "Sorry, can you sign for these samples?" as if their time wasn't as valuable as the doctor's or their products weren't worth a quick discussion. By apologizing, these reps undermined their role as trusted and valued advisors and positioned themselves more as delivery people. The doctors treated them accordingly, with less respect.

To improve their relationships with the doctors and enhance the perception of our company, these reps needed more confidence in the value of their role. Had they been sure of the value they were bringing, through their expertise, experience, and products, they would have been perceived totally differently. The first step in changing that perception was to stop apologizing.

> When you apologize, it devalues your contribution and puts you in an inferior position—not where a leader should be. By offering apologies only when they are warranted, you keep them meaningful and retain your rank as leader.

CONFIDENCE BREEDS LEADERS

To eliminate unnecessary apologies that damage your leadership ability and your reputation, start by examining when you say "I'm sorry" and then reflecting on what you're apologizing for. You'll be surprised at how often you use the phrase. Once you have identified the situations in which you overapologize, the next step is working on your confidence level. When you feel good about your level of performance, whether on the golf course or in the boardroom, you find fewer reasons to apologize. If you've done your best, why should you say "I'm sorry"?

CHAPTER SUMMARY POINTS

- "I'm sorry" is one of the most overused phrases in the English language. In many cases, it doesn't accurately reflect what the speaker meant, but is used in place of a phrase such as "excuse me" or said because of misplaced guilt.

- Women have a habit of using "I'm sorry" as a conversation starter, and this immediately undervalues their position. Don't start out at a disadvantage by apologizing unnecessarily, as Angie witnessed with her colleagues in pharmaceutical sales. Reps who began their sales pitch with "I'm sorry" positioned themselves as people undeserving of the doctors' time rather than as leaders who had solutions to the doctors' problems.

- Leaders apologize only when they are truly at fault for something, such as missing a deadline or failing to handle an important situation. Corporal Nguyen, for example, said "I'm sorry" after he had lost equipment that he was responsible for, but he didn't go overboard, and he made sure that it was one of the few instances in which he ever had to apologize for a mistake; thus, his apology was valuable.

- If you find yourself apologizing frequently, it could be a sign that you're overcommitted and therefore are unable to perform at your best. And if that's the case, you can address the situation by pulling back and refocusing your efforts on your top priorities.

- Apologies are also used to diffuse tense situations or to avoid confrontations. The problem is that when you avoid heated discussions, you may never address the underlying situation and discover a solution. Angie's habit of apologizing to end arguments with her husband served only to leave the arguments unresolved and ready to come up again later. By working through the difficult issues, rather than apologizing and walking away, Angie and Matt came to solutions and strengthened their relationship.

- Limiting your use of apologies to situations that are truly your fault will strengthen your standing as a leader and keep you focused on what you need to do to achieve success. Apologies have a way of limiting your progress by taking your attention away from what's truly important. Sergeant Reynolds, for example, said "I'm sorry" constantly and damaged his leadership potential. Instead of looking for ways to improve, he relied on apologies to cover his underperformance. As a result, he didn't improve and his career stalled.

CHAPTER 10

ALWAYS LEAD AS YOU ARE

Becoming a leader doesn't require you to overhaul your personality or change your personal style. In fact, the things that make you special and unique will make you a better leader. To be effective, you need to work on enhancing your strengths and improving your weaknesses. You may need to learn some new behaviors, like holding back tears, or cutting back on others, such as placing blame elsewhere, but never try to be someone you're not.

We've had countless women ask us how they can maintain their identity when everyone around them is trying to change them. Many of them have heard from their superiors that some aspect of their behavior needs to change, such as their style of dress or their habit of procrastinating, and they interpret that to mean that they need to change their personality. The truth is, you shouldn't try to change your personality—who you are inside—you can improve your performance by being the real you.

You can't act the part of a leader or mimic someone else's leadership style and be a good leader. For example, acting more masculine or stern, when your true nature is feminine or light-hearted, will only make you uncomfortable. Plus, you'll come across as phony or a fake because being stern is not who you really are. Those you are leading will be able to see right through your façade, and you will lose their respect. The energy you expend in trying to be someone you're not would be much better invested in enhancing your true gifts—what makes you who you are.

We've heard from many women in our audiences that there is nothing they hate more than seeing a colleague be suddenly transformed from a friend into a "bitch" after a promotion. They wonder aloud why their peers believe they need to morph into strict, humorless taskmasters in order to get things done, when they were promoted based on who they really are. The only reasonable explanation for this sudden change that we've been able to come up with is that the women who do this mistakenly believe that it's expected of them.

Why waste your time and effort attempting to be aloof if your sense of caring is one of your best personality traits? Or why try to rid yourself of your sensitivity if that ability has gotten you where you are today? Don't try to hide your true personality, leverage it to help you become a better leader.

That means taking stock of your strengths and weaknesses and being aware of what you may need to do to compensate for those weaknesses. If you're a shy person, being a leader doesn't require that you suddenly morph into an outgoing, gregarious person. However, it does require that you make an effort to speak up and let those around you know that you're there to support them. Or if you have a sense of humor, don't try to cover it up—use it. Your team will appreciate it, and you, that much more.

One of the greatest misconceptions about Marines is that they are cookie-cutter warriors, each like all the rest. They're not, and we hope you've seen that in the examples throughout this book. The Marine Corps is full of individuals with unique talents and abilities, and the organization is stronger because of those differences. If everyone were the same, the Corps would be much weaker. Instead, the Marine Corps has perfected the art of helping all members recognize their full potential as leaders by encouraging them to remain authentic.

We went through the indoctrination process in the Corps, and instead of being transformed into carbon copies of other Marines, as some of our friends and family members feared we might, we became stronger versions of ourselves. We became confident leaders. And like our fellow Marines, we used our unique personalities to influence outcomes and inspire others.

Courtney learned the importance of individuality from an experienced Marine who quickly brought clarity to a confusing situation.

DON'T CHANGE WHO YOU ARE

Courtney

Despite having been told the importance of being genuine—of letting your true personality come out—when leading others, I saw many newly minted Marine officers struggle with their new identity as leaders. Some were just out of college, and perhaps were not yet comfortable with supervising 50 Marines right off the bat; they thought they needed to act more "like a boss." To them, that meant adopting a more serious, unflinching demeanor—a "never let them see you smile" attitude—or trying to lower their voices to sound more authoritative. While they thought it was necessary to act the part of an officer in charge, they were really losing credibility with everyone around them. It was obvious that they were playing the part of a leader rather than being one.

Early in my Marine Corps career, there came one of the rare occasions when I reported to another woman, Captain Roberts. This was also the only time someone in the Corps ever asked me to change my personality. A talented officer, Captain Roberts's one weakness was her practice of assuming a masculine demeanor when her subordinates were around. She equated leadership with men, apparently, and felt the need to model their behavior in order to fit into the Marine Corps, which, in fact, is more of a man's world.

While she believed that acting this way helped her earn the respect of those around her, it was actually damaging her credibility. Many of my peers, and hers, too, snickered at her attempts to be tough and rigid when her true personality was anything but; she was insincere, and it was obvious to everyone, including me. But her behavior didn't really bother me (if she wanted to pretend to be manly, that was OK with me) until she began encouraging me to assume a masculine demeanor as well. She told me that she wanted me to succeed as an officer and that she believed that if I acted more like my male peers, I would have a better chance of success.

Her recommendation—an order, really—confused me.

"Lieutenant, if you'd stomp out your 'smoking and joking' attitude, you'd really go places," Captain Roberts told me.

"Yes, Ma'am," was all I could muster, since I wasn't sure what she was referring to.

"Your lackadaisical attitude is hurting your career, Lieutenant. You need to get serious and show your Marines that you mean business," she told me.

"Yes, Ma'am," was, again, all I could think of. Sure, I was laid back, but that was my personality. In times of stress, I compensated for my unease with a positive attitude. It appeared that Captain Roberts was misinterpreting my smiles. But I had no idea how to squelch my personality.

Did the Marine Corps really want me to change? My boss was telling me to do something that didn't feel right, but I wasn't really sure I could be more tough and rigid; it just wasn't me. If I gave in to the captain's demand that I change who I was for the sake of fitting into the Corps, I knew there was a good chance that I'd lose credibility. But if I didn't obey her, I might damage my career prospects.

What I didn't know was that as I was struggling with Captain Roberts's counsel, Colonel Carl Jackson—the commanding officer of our entire unit—had heard about Captain Roberts's efforts to change me. He had read some of the informal evaluations Captain Roberts had written about me and was concerned. So he summoned me to his office one afternoon. It was unheard of for a young, junior officer to be asked to go to the colonel's office, so I was nervous. Had I done something wrong?

When I arrived at the colonel's office, I announced my presence and stood at attention. The colonel immediately told me to stand at ease and did all he could to make me feel comfortable, perhaps realizing how nervous I was. "Lieutenant," he said, "you know what I love about the Marine Corps?"

"No, sir," I responded.

"I love the fact that the Corps is big enough for all kinds of characters. Characters like me and characters like you, Lieutenant," he continued. "When you are out there with your troops, you stay true to who you are. The Corps needs you to be a leader, and you are a leader as you are. Don't change who you are for anybody or anything. In order to be effective, you have to lead as you are. Do you understand that, Lieutenant?" he asked.

"Yes, sir," I responded, a smile crossing my face.

"Very well, then, you are dismissed," he told me.

With that one brief discussion, the colonel taught me a lesson that stays with me today. Without ever mentioning Captain Roberts—after all, discretion is the better part of valor—he let me know that there will always be people who want to change you. But in the end, you really can't change who you are—and shouldn't try. Instead, accent and develop your strengths as you work on improving or dealing with your weaknesses. But remember: improving yourself doesn't mean changing who you are.

> Don't fundamentally change who you are to match your organization's image—doing so won't allow you to demonstrate your true personality and strengths. Pretending to be someone you are not is not leadership behavior. Remaining true to your personality while serving as a role model for others is.

Angie learned this lesson on a Navy ship en route to Puerto Rico. She didn't need to change who she was to be a more effective leader, but she did need to work through her weaknesses—namely, her lack of self-confidence.

PLAYING THE PART ISN'T ENOUGH

Angie

When people are in a new situation, they often create a façade in order to fit in. They behave the way they think they should in order to be liked by those around them. When I was 19, I experienced this firsthand during a tour aboard a Navy ship as part of my ROTC training.

I spent three weeks aboard a ship in order to learn more about the roles of Marines and sailors and to study ship systems, field tactics, and other aspects of the Navy and Marine Corps. There were a total of 450 sailors and Marines on the ship, and only 20 were women. I was not yet an officer, but was about to become one. I was serving alongside well-prepared Marines and sailors whom I would eventually be tasked with leading. Back at college, I had found my place in the midshipman battalion as a leader in training, but the ship was new territory, and I wasn't sure how to act on my first day.

I reported to Norfolk, Virginia, wearing my Navy white uniform. I looked the part of a Naval midshipman, but I felt that I was play-acting. As I stared up at the enormous vessel, all I could do was ask myself what I was doing here. This was the real deal—the first time I would be working alongside active-duty military men and women—and it was my opportunity to see how I would fit in. I would either thrive and prove myself as a capable future Marine officer, or struggle and potentially fail. I was extremely nervous about the experience I was about to have.

I was the first to arrive, before the other midshipmen, so I had to try to recall on my own the correct protocol for boarding a ship, such as saluting the National Ensign—the flag at back of the ship—and then the officer of the day. I had no idea if I was doing it properly, which shook my confidence a little. I was also very much aware of my status as a glorified college trainee—I was the poster child for the term *rookie*—and felt as if all eyes were watching to determine whether I deserved to wear the uniform I had on.

One of the first sailors I met asked if I knew my way to the area where I could "drop my gear." I confessed to him that I had never been on a ship before, and, luckily, he escorted me through a maze of steel ladders and passageways to my berthing area, where I was going to sleep. The ship was so enormous that you could literally get lost for hours trying to find your way around.

I was relieved when the other midshipmen began to arrive, and grateful that there were Naval Academy students onboard. If anyone knew about Navy vessels, it had to be the Naval Academy students, so I decided to stick close to them to learn from their experience. The good news was that these students were very comfortable being on the ship, but the bad news was that I began to feel insecure about my own knowledge of the Navy and Marines; compared to them, I felt like I knew very little. (The Marine Corps, while a separate branch of the armed forces, is still part of the Department of the Navy.)

As we got underway, I watched closely as the Naval Academy midshipmen made their way through the ship, dealing with the officers and enlisted personnel with confidence. Their comfort level had a disastrous effect on my self-esteem: the more I compared myself to them, the less prepared and the less qualified I felt. Where they could have an intelligent conversation with the officers and enlisted personnel, I found myself tongue-tied and unsure. They understood the technical aspects of the ship's functioning, knew the protocols for embarking and debarking, and knew the right questions to ask. I began to wonder if I even belonged there.

Since I felt that I had so little to contribute, I decided that my best strategy would be to lie low and watch and learn from the Naval Academy midshipmen, in hopes that I could ultimately be like them. I spent a lot of time listening to them, rather than participating in a discussion and sharing what I knew; I put my own thoughts and opinions on the back burner. I stopped speaking out, stopped being assertive, and second-guessed myself at every turn. Within a few short weeks, I went from being a confident, self-assured college junior to an insecure, mousy midshipman, all in an effort to be like those around me.

Then one day another midshipman, Tim Gomez, and I were working together with the electrician's mate. Neither of us was particularly thrilled with our assignment, and we took frequent opportunities to sneak out to the ship's deck and goof off, looking out into the sea for dolphins. Tim was an English major, like me, and we began talking about our favorite books. When he asked what my all-time favorite book was, I told him it had to be *Beloved*, by Toni Morrison. I had just taken an American literature class the previous semester and had fallen in love with the story. But I told him about other authors I enjoyed, too, like Steinbeck and Hemingway, and mentioned that many of Hemingway's stories took place in the area where I grew up. As I went on about my interest in reading, he looked at me with curiosity. I could sense that he seemed surprised by what I'd said, but I wasn't sure why.

"What's up? Are you an English major who doesn't like to read?" I asked with a smile. He appeared taken aback.

"Well, don't take this the wrong way," he said, "but I thought you were an airhead. I'm kind of surprised you know so much about literature."

I was shocked. No one had ever accused me of being an airhead, and in a million years I wouldn't have described myself that way. I saw myself as determined, assertive, intelligent, and funny. Airhead? No way.

He also confided that other midshipmen thought I was flighty, too.

Although it stung to hear that others' perception of me didn't match my own self-image, I was grateful to Tim for sharing everyone's take on me. His confession shocked me into taking a hard look at the way I'd been behaving, and he was right. I had been acting like an airhead. Instead of asking questions in order to learn more or speaking out to show what I did know, I had opted to try to blend into the crowd. I had been more concerned about fitting in and being liked than about being authentic. Along the way, I lost myself and my identity.

My discomfort in my new environment had obviously made me uncomfortable with myself. And if Tim and his friends saw me as a ditz, it was likely that the sailors and Marines I was working alongside also saw me as a ditz. What's worse, because there were only 20 women onboard, I was probably creating a terrible image of female Marines. In the Marines, (and in life) airheads don't get respect; they get walked over. I didn't want this to happen to me.

I had created a façade to hide behind, thinking that it would help compensate for my insecurities. But Tim's comment about my reputation helped me see that the façade I had created was damaging my reputation, not helping it. I also recognized that sometimes there is a trade-off between being liked and being respected. I had been so focused on being liked that I had discounted the importance of respect. Now I decided that I'd rather be respected for who I am than liked for who I am not.

When I dropped the façade I had created, I started to relax and enjoy myself. I also opened up a bit more and introduced my fellow midshipmen, as well as the Marines and sailors, to the real me—the Angie I knew, respected, and liked. Ultimately, they grew to respect and like the real me, too.

> When you try to change your personality to become more likable, you lose respect and credibility. You're not a leader in that situation because you're not being true to who you are. The more authentic you are, the more likely it is that you will earn the respect of others.

DON'T ASPIRE TO FIT THE MOLD

Courtney

When I reentered the private sector after serving as a Marine, I was different—different from the young woman who had entered the Corps four years before, and different from my coworkers at the software company. For one thing, I wasn't a trendy dresser; after years of wearing a uniform day in and day out, I wasn't up on the latest styles. For another, unlike my peers, I had the benefit of formal leadership training.

I walked into an environment full of successful, put together professionals, most of whom were between 28 and 45. At 25, I was several years younger than the youngest people at the company. No one else had military experience, and, I suspected, some didn't understand the value of such service. Everyone in the sales department was obviously doing well financially, as evidenced by the fancy cars in the parking lot and the Prada shoes on their feet. In contrast, I drove a beat-up Honda and preferred comfortable footwear. I also didn't have the free time they did—I was beginning law school and had just become my grandmother's caregiver. My life felt quite different from the lives of my new coworkers.

My insecurity about my new job and the differences I perceived between my colleagues and me was confusing. After the Marines I didn't expect a new job to shake my confidence. Surprisingly, I began to doubt my abilities. I got so caught up in outward appearances that I felt left out and unpopular, and I temporarily forgot what it was that had earned me the job in the first place—my leadership skills.

Fortunately, my leadership training helped me get back on track quickly. Recalling the wisdom of Marines like Colonel Jackson, who had impressed on me the importance of leading as I was, I psyched myself up each day before going to the office. I worked on developing my own sense of style, which was a step up from what I had previously worn, but didn't quite approach the stylish attire of my coworkers. I also worked to really get to know my colleagues, rather than continuing to be intimidated by their appearance. By having lunches with the "beautiful people," I realized that they were just that—inside and out. And, surprisingly, we had a lot in common. I'm proud to still call many of them good friends today. After getting past my initial assumption that what made me different made me inferior, I realized that those differences were actually an advantage.

I learned many things from the people I worked with as a result of getting to know them. Plus, I was able to share my strengths as a person and as a leader. A few months after starting at the company, I was promoted to a management position. I was the youngest manager by about 10 years and the only female manager in the 13-state region I was part of. I was promoted because I was a strong performer. My managers noticed that I was an authentic, credible person who had an ability to influence outcomes and inspire others. I was a leader.

When faced with challenges, it's natural to have insecurities, but the true test of a leader is how he or she handles them. Had I allowed my initial self-doubt to fester, it's likely that I would have donned a façade to try to fit in. I would have wasted incredible amounts of energy trying to be someone I wasn't, ignoring the years of leadership training I had received that had taught me the importance of leading as I was. And instead of fitting in and gaining credibility within the company, I would have lost it all—credibility, respect, and my promotion. Instead, by staying true to who I was, I focused on letting others get to know the real me and making an effort to get to know them, too.

> Have confidence in your unique talents and experiences. These qualities form the basis of your leadership style and allow you to be the strongest leader you can be.

YOU CAN'T LEAD AS YOU ARE
UNTIL YOU KNOW WHO YOU ARE

Like success, leadership is a journey, not a destination. You don't suddenly arrive at being a leader—it's a process of developing your character and your skills. As a leader, you continuously assess where you are, where you're headed, and what opportunities for improvement you have. You recognize and are proud of your strengths, which bolster your self-esteem, and you acknowledge your weaknesses, which you are regularly working to improve.

What makes you different makes you strong, although that's not always our first assumption. Perhaps because many of us were teased in junior high school for being different, we equate sameness with strength, with popularity, and with power. But aiming to be just like everyone else isn't much of a goal—being different is. Differences make teams strong and, when combined with solid leadership and an ability to work well together, make us successful.

It's also important to note that leading as you are doesn't mean staying as you currently are forever. Self-improvement and exploration are also signs of a leader, and they start with self-evaluation. Assessing your strengths and weaknesses helps you identify opportunities for improvement that can have an impact on your career and personal life.

One of the best ways to conduct a self-evaluation is simply to spend time by yourself and reflect. Think about what you enjoy, both at work and in your spare time, and what you don't, in terms of both tasks or activities and people. Contemplate where your life is headed: Where do you see yourself in a year? How about in three? Are you taking actions that will help you get there?

Scheduling an hour or so for yourself once a week is a good way to check in with your psyche. Are you happy with your life? What would you change? How would you change it? And what would your first step be? These are all issues you should be thinking about regularly, to get yourself on track for success.

The good news is that as you improve, as you make progress toward your goals, you will feel better about yourself. Your confidence will grow, making you more eager to work on self-improvement—it becomes a positive cycle, and you move closer to achieving your goals.

Your confidence also helps you recognize the strengths of others. You feel less jealousy and envy when you feel good about yourself, and this makes you a better leader.

In addition to self-evaluations, listening to feedback from those around you (solicited and unsolicited) is another tool for developing your potential. You receive feedback informally, such as from your spouse's suggestion that you may want to rethink wearing a bright pink booty skirt to your cousin's wedding (or anywhere else, for that matter), and you receive it more formally, such as through a performance appraisal at work or your credit score, which summarizes your financial health.

Of course, feedback reflects how others perceive you, not necessarily how you truly are. This means that while you should accept the information offered, you don't necessarily need to act on it. But feedback is useful for assessing how closely your outward persona matches your internal one, so that you can make the changes that will bring them into alignment with your role as a leader.

ACTING ON FEEDBACK IS OPTIONAL

Angie

I've always used formal performance evaluations as tools to help me improve myself professionally. Granted, I may not always agree with the way I'm being perceived by my superiors, but it's still useful to have someone suggest ways in which I can improve. I found this particularly valuable in a fast-paced job where I was trying to figure out how to meet my boss's expectations.

My manager at one of the pharmaceutical companies where I was employed told me that she had hired me because I was a Marine. To her, that meant that I would be aggressive, and she wanted an aggressive salesperson. However, I'm reserved, and I equate the term *aggressive* with an "in your face" personality, which I don't have.

Although my personality fit fine in the Marine Corps, I was beginning to think I might not have met my boss's initial expectations. So when, during a performance evaluation, she revealed her desire for more aggressive behavior on my part, I wasn't surprised. Still, I pushed her to clarify what she meant by the term, since I had always viewed being aggressive as a negative. Did she think I needed to set up more sales presentations? Was she expecting me to be bolder, more pushy, during sales calls? I wanted to be the best pharmaceutical sales rep I could be, and if there was something she had observed that could help me improve, I wanted to hear about it. I tried to get to the heart of what she really meant. By remaining calm and asking several follow-up questions to get to the root of the behavior she wanted to see, I realized that she didn't think I was effective at closing calls—essentially, asking clients for the business. This was a realistic coaching point that wouldn't require me to alter my personality.

She didn't want me to bully the doctor into buying from me (which I consider aggressive behavior), but she did want me to gain commitment and ask the doctor to prescribe my company's products. Like most new sales reps, I found this last step to be the most uncomfortable and the one I liked least, so it was no wonder that I wanted to gloss right over it. But her evaluation showed me the importance of taking this step, of closing the sale.

It also showed me that to meet her expectation, I didn't need to change who I was and to become more aggressive—I just needed to improve my closing skills on sales calls. Feedback is most useful when you learn steps that you can take to build specific skills; it's less valuable when you're told to somehow alter your personality. It's generally not worth the effort to attempt that.

By taking time to understand my boss's comments, I was able to improve my performance. I became more confident in my role as a sales rep, and I became more effective, but I didn't become more aggressive. I focused on specific things I could do to meet my boss's expectations without worrying about changing aspects of my personality that were simply unchangeable. Working on asking for the sale helped me become a better salesperson—stepping outside my comfort zone improved my performance without changing my personality.

> Be open to receiving critical feedback; yet if it seems to conflict with your personality don't act on it, instead seek clarification. Take time and question feedback so that you know what skills need improvement, instead of trying to change your personality to fit someone else's perceptions.

LEAD FROM A POSITION OF STRENGTH

When we joined the Marines, we were both somewhat surprised to learn that there is no one way of being a Marine Corps leader. We thought we would be trained to think or act in a specific way—the Marine Corps way. Instead, the Corps didn't try to change our personalities or force us to conform; rather, it challenged us to be the best we could be by encouraging us to bolster our strengths and improve on our weaknesses.

Some of the best, most important lessons we took away from the Corps were those that showed us that we had the talent, determination, and strength to achieve much more than we had ever thought we could. We learned that, if you let it, your mind can significantly limit your body and your spirit. One of our drill instructors at Officer Candidate School used to say, "Mind over matter, candidates. If you don't mind, it don't matter." She'd usually offer this motivation as we were about to submerge ourselves in mud, engage in hand-to-hand combat, or step off on a long-distance run—physically demanding tasks that we might have wondered if we could complete. And her simple reminder let us know that our mind was there to *help us* get through anything. We learned that you can do anything in life—don't ever let yourself or any other person or circumstance make you believe otherwise.

Becoming Marines and becoming leaders required us to let go of all the limitations we had unknowingly placed on ourselves or had let others place on us. Looking back on our military careers, it's hard to believe some of the feats we survived and the amazing experiences we had. From routine 20-mile hikes to rappelling down a 500-foot cliff, to slipping out of a massive ship's cargo hold on a small troop boat at the crack of dawn, to dining with the prime minister of Japan, to answering the questions of the press at the Pentagon, to leading Marines on a formation run proudly calling cadence, to deploying to foreign lands and offering humanitarian support, to working hard to make a difference in the lives of others—the list goes on and on.

Before we became leaders with the Marine Corps' help, we weren't nearly as confident or as sure of who we were as we are now. But believing in ourselves and pushing beyond our comfort zones from time to time expanded our minds, our bodies, and our confidence. Fortunately, you don't need to join the Marine Corps to have those kinds of exhilarating but terrifying experiences. What you need to do is value your uniqueness and always look for opportunities to improve and to live the life you want to live.

LEAD FROM THE FRONT

We learned to lead from the front in the Marine Corps and carried that knowledge into successful careers in the private sector—Angie in the pharmaceutical industry and Courtney in software and law—after making the difficult decision to leave the Corps. For both of us, that decision came down to the fact that we had accomplished all the goals we had set out to achieve at the beginning of our military careers. After ROTC and active-duty service, Angie felt that she had done everything she wanted to do in the military and was ready for a new challenge in a civilian job. Courtney also treasured her Marine Corps experience, but was ready to pursue her lifelong dream of attending law school, which the Corps had made possible through the GI Bill. Both of us were honorably discharged and sad to go, but ready for new leadership challenges. Fortunately, once a Marine, always a Marine—our experiences in the Corps continue to affect and influence us on a daily basis.

Being able to lead from the front proved to be a distinct advantage for us—more than we ever imagined. We now lead balanced lives, enjoying time with those we love while being able to establish our own priorities. Ultimately our leadership know-how has led us to start our own leadership consulting firm, Lead Star, in an effort to further our desire to share leadership wisdom with women everywhere.

We're proof that these leadership lessons work, and that you, too, can achieve the success you want. All it takes is the decision to lead your life from the front, every day. And we know you can do that. When you lead the life you want to live, you'll become a stronger, more authentic version of yourself. You'll lead your life, rather than being led by your life's circumstances. By becoming a leader, you'll bring the best parts of yourself to light.

As soon as you start living the leadership principles you've learned in this book, you'll be amazed at how your life will start to change. You'll see how powerful you feel as you make the changes you've wanted to make. Others will look to you for guidance and inspiration. When you lead from the front, you'll have the honor and opportunity to serve those around you. You'll also have the ability to influence outcomes and inspire others in ways that will make a positive difference.

Congratulations!

CHAPTER SUMMARY POINTS

• Being an effective leader does not require you to change some aspect of your personality, or to pretend to be someone you're not. The best leaders lead as they are. This point was made clear to Courtney by her Marine Corps boss, who discouraged her from adopting mannerisms typically associated with Marine Corps leaders, most of whom were male.

- People who assume some alternative persona, or façade, that they think represents what a leader looks and acts like aren't leaders. They're wanna-bes—and ineffective ones at that. Putting on an act takes too much time and energy and causes you to lose the respect of those around you. Simply be who you are and you'll be a leader. Angie learned the hard way that a façade can backfire and hide your greatest qualities—you should just be yourself.

- Becoming a leader is an ongoing process, rather than a particular milestone. The best leaders are constantly working to further improve their skills and abilities, constantly trying to improve themselves. Asking for feedback from your boss, as Angie did, can help you zero in on improving specific aspects of your performance, so that you can be a better employee and a better leader.

- To know what skills or traits you should be working on, set aside time on a regular basis to do a self-assessment. Reflect on your strengths and your weaknesses. Then contemplate what you could do short term and long term to address them.

- Asking for and listening to feedback from people you trust can also be helpful. But put anyone's counsel into perspective. Just because someone offers criticism does not mean that you need to follow that person's advice. Consider the input without becoming defensive so that you'll be able to recognize self-improvement tips that you might not have thought of.

- Don't try to hide what makes you different, whether it's your love of public speaking, your immense hat collection, or your expert scrapbooking know-how. What makes you different will make you a better leader.

INDEX

ABOUT THE AUTHORS

Angie Morgan

Angie Morgan is a leader, an entrepreneur, a sought-after speaker, and cofounder of Lead Star, LLC. A graduate of the University of Michigan and a life-long Wolverine fan, Angie is committed to sparking a national dialogue on the subject of women and leadership. She is also an avid runner and enjoys reading books to her son, Judge Daniel. You can e-mail Angie at amorgan@leadingfromthefront.com.

Courtney Lynch

Courtney Lynch is a leader, a successful business owner, an accomplished speaker, and cofounder of Lead Star, LLC. After graduating from North Carolina State University, Courtney earned her law degree from William & Mary School of Law. She is passionate about helping others develop their leadership skills. When she's not traveling the country providing leadership workshops, Courtney enjoys skiing, reading, and spending time with her family and friends. To contact Courtney, e-mail her at clynch@leadingfromthefront.com.